The
Population
of Malaysia

The **Institute of Southeast Asian Studies (ISEAS)** was established as an autonomous organization in 1968. It is a regional centre dedicated to the study of socio-political, security and economic trends and developments in Southeast Asia and its wider geostrategic and economic environment.

The Institute's research programmes are the Regional Economic Studies (RES, including ASEAN and APEC), Regional Strategic and Political Studies (RSPS), and Regional Social and Cultural Studies (RSCS).

ISEAS Publishing, an established academic press, has issued almost 2,000 books and journals. It is the largest scholarly publisher of research about Southeast Asia from within the region. ISEAS Publishing works with many other academic and trade publishers and distributors to disseminate important research and analyses from and about Southeast Asia to the rest of the world.

Saw Swee-Hock

The Population of Malaysia

LSEAS Institute of Southeast Asian Studies
Singapore

First published in Singapore in 2007 by ISEAS Publishing
Institute of Southeast Asian Studies
30 Heng Mui Keng Terrace
Pasir Panjang
Singapore 119614

E-mail: publish@iseas.edu.sg
Website: <http://bookshop.iseas.edu.sg>

This book is published under ISEAS Malaysia Study Programme funded by Professor Saw Swee-Hock.

ISEAS Library Cataloguing-in-Publication Data

Saw Swee-Hock, 1931–
   The population of Malaysia.
   1. Demography—Malaysia.
   2. Malaysia—Population.
   I. Title
HB3644.6 A3S371   2007

ISBN: 978-981-230-443-8 (hard cover)
ISBN: 978-981-230-728-6 (PDF)

Typeset by Superskill Graphics Pte Ltd
Printed in Singapore by Photoplates Pte Ltd

Contents

List of Tables

List of Figures

Preface

This book, a project of the Malaysia Study Programme of ISEAS, is a sequel to my earlier book on *The Population of Peninsular Malaysia* published some time ago in 1988 and just reprinted by ISEAS in 2007. The old book was essentially based on materials derived from the early population censuses and other relevant sources pertaining to the eleven states of West Malaysia. It was not feasible to include Sabah and Sarawak in the book considering the extreme paucity of comparable data for these two eastern states for the period under study.

The situation has improved quite significantly following the formation of Malaysia in 1963 when a wide range of pan-Malaysia statistics was made available from the four population censuses held since 1970 and from other sources dealing with vital events, labour force, etc. The emergence of favourable conditions has enabled me to bring out a completely different book covering the entire country rather than a second edition of the original book. In writing this new book on *The Population of Malaysia*, I have been guided by the need to present a comprehensive analysis of the demographic trends and patterns discernable in the multiracial country during the last four decades or so.

I would like to acknowledge the assistance of numerous institutions and individuals. For helping me to access the research materials, my thanks go to the University of Malaya Library, the National University of Singapore Library, ISEAS Library and the London School of Economics Library where I visited during my frequent visits to London. My special thanks go to the Malaysian Department of Statistics for willingly supplying the necessary data. I would like to thank Ambassador K. Kesavapany, Director of ISEAS, for his encouragement and hospitality, and Mrs Triena Ong of ISEAS Publications Unit for overseeing the expeditious publication of the book. Needless to say, any opinions and shortcomings in the book are my own.

Saw Swee-Hock
October 2006

1

Introduction

GEOGRAPHICAL SETTING

Malaysia consists of two distinct geographical segments separated by the South China Sea, Peninsular (or West) Malaysia in the west and east Malaysia in the east. The long narrow peninsula of West Malaysia extends from latitude 1° 20' north to latitude 6° 40' north, and from longitude 99° 35' to longitude 104° 20' east. It is situated in a central position within Southeast Asia, being an extension of the Asian land mass as well as part of the wider Malay archipelago. Beyond Peninsular Malaysia's northern land border lies Thailand, and its immediate neighbour in the south is the small island state of Singapore joined to it by the old rail-and-road causeway and the new second-link bridge, both cutting through the narrow Straits of Johore. In the west just across the busy Straits of Malacca is the large elongated island of Sumatra, part of the multi-island Republic of Indonesia.

East Malaysia occupies the north and north-west portion of the huge island of Borneo. It extends from latitude 0° 85' north to latitude 7° 35' north, and from longitude 109° 60' to longitude 119° 35' east. To the south, it shares a common land border with Kalimantan which is an Indonesian territory, and in the north across the Sulu Sea is the Republic of the Philippines. Because of its proximity, the people have considerable contacts with these two neighbours, perhaps more so than with Peninsular Malaysia. Though East Malaysia has a land area of 198,160 square kilometres that is larger than the 132,090 in West Malaysia, it is not that important viewed from many aspects. For one thing, it contains only two states, Sabah and Sarawak as compared to the eleven states and the Federal Territory of Kuala Lumpur, the hub of the Federal Government, in Peninsular Malaysia.

Peninsular Malaysia extends some 740 kilometres in length from Perlis state in the north to Johore Bahru town in the south, and about 322 kilometres in width at its widest point. The total land area approximates 132,090 square kilometres, slightly larger than England without Wales. It has a coastline of nearly 1,931 kilometres, covered in many places with mangrove swamps, sand bars and sandy beaches. The western side has a few natural harbours but the eastern coastline is rather shallow, sandy and without good harbours. The country comprises a series of mountain ranges running from the northwest in the Thai border to southwest into the state of Negri Sembilan. To the west of this central range is the Bintang Range extending from the northern border to the Taiping region, while to the east is an area of highland in Kelantan and Trengganu. These main mountain masses determine the drainage system which is well served by a multiplicity of rivers, somewhat shorter and more numerous in the west. The rivers are narrow and swift in their upper reaches but become sluggish and meandering once they enter the coastal plains. They have been the chief means of communication and important factors in the growth of settlements and towns.

Much of East Malaysia is mountainous. In Sabah the Crocker Range, with the 4,100-metre high Mount Kinabalu in the northern end, runs parallel to the west coast. There are other smaller mountain complexes in various localities in the east. In Sarawak the highest point is less than 2,500 metres, but there are large areas with mountainous terrain. The longest river in Sabah, Kinabatangan River, flows from the centre to the east, while the Rajang River in Sarawak travelled from east to west. In both states, the vast network of rivers constitutes a prominent feature of the landscape and serves as an important means of transport. Both states have considerable patches of mangrove swamps along the long coastline, some 1,450 kilometres in Sabah and 810 kilometres in Sarawak.

Malaysia, being near the tropics, has most of its land mass covered with dense tropical forests and exposed to an equatorial climate with uniform and high temperatures, abundant rainfall and high humidity. Temperatures are constantly high throughout the year, with only slight changes in the average monthly temperatures. Somewhat greater variations are shown by the daily temperatures which may fluctuate between 22 to 32 degrees inland. The rainy seasons are very much influenced by the southwest and the northeast monsoons. During the northeast monsoon in October to March, the east coast of Peninsular

Malaysia and the west coast of East Malaysia are exposed to heavy rain. The southwest monsoon in April to September brings heavy rain to particularly the western coastal belt of Peninsular Malaysia. Fairly frequent convectional rain occurs during the two inter-monsoon periods, thunderstorms are not infrequent all the year round.

HISTORICAL BACKGROUND

Before the coming of the Europeans in the early sixteenth century, the territory now known as Peninsular Malaysia, was under the rule of various Malay sultanates established at different periods in the west coast, especially around Malacca.[1] Prior to this the country was under the sway of the Majapahit Empire centred in Java which had earlier replaced the Sri Vijaya Empire in the fourteenth century. The first European incursion into the country occurred in 1511 when the Portuguese captured Malacca and held sway until it was in turn captured by the Dutch in 1641. The Dutch ruled Malacca until the late eighteenth century when the British took over. In 1786 Francis Light occupied the island of Penang on behalf of the East India Company, and the island together with the hinterland of Province Wellesley were ceded to the company. A decade later in 1795, Malacca was surrendered by the Dutch to the British and, though returned on two occasions, was eventually given to the British in 1825 in exchange for Bencoolen. Further south the settlement of Singapore was established by Stamford Raffles for the East India Company in 1819.

In 1826 the three British possessions of Penang, Malacca and Singapore were combined into one administrative unit known as the Straits Settlements, which was subsequently transferred from the control of the East India Company to the Colonial Office in 1867. British influence did not stop here. The increasing interest of the British in the affairs of the hinterland Malay States resulted in the four central states of Perak, Selangor, Negri Sembilan, and Pahang accepting British control and coming together to form the Federated Malay States in 1895. This larger political unit had a centralised form of government, with a British Resident in each state. In theory the British Residents were supposed to advise the Rulers, but in practice their advice must be accepted if it had nothing to do with Malay customs and religion. The other five states, Perlis, Kedah, Kelantan, Trengganu and Johore, remained outside the two larger political groupings, and were frequently referred to, rather accusingly, as the Unfederated Malay States. They were each administered with the aid of a British Adviser as a separate political entity. This broad political framework continued to exist right up to the outbreak of war in December 1941, culminating in the Japanese Occupation of the country from February 1942 to September 1945.

The early postwar period saw some swift and profound political changes. The first government to take control of the country after the war was the British Military Administration whose prime task was to restore law and order. This temporary military administration was replaced by the creation of the Malayan Union on 1 April 1946, incorporating all the states, except Singapore, under a Governor and a strong central government. Since the new constitution deprived the Rulers of all their important powers, it evoked the resentment of the people, especially the Malays. The Malayan Union was thus abandoned in favour of the Federation of Malaya on 1 February 1948. Under this new constitutional framework the Malay Rulers remained sovereign in the nine Malay states, while Penang and Malacca were administered as British territories. Singapore was excluded from the Federation and was governed as a separate British colony. A significant feature of the new agreement is that, with the consensus of the British Crown and the Malay Rulers, provisions for progress towards eventual self-government were included.

On 1 August 1957 the Federation of Malaya became a free and independent country under a Yang Di-Pertuan Agong elected every five years from among the nine Rulers. Each state has an elected state legislature, while the federal legislature consists of a senate and a house of representatives which had fully elected members. In the election held after independence the Alliance, which comprised the United Malay National Organisation (UMNO), the Malayan Chinese Association (MCA), and the Malayan Indian Congress (MIC), was voted into power. The Alliance, under the premiership of Tengku Abdul Rahman, formed the first independent government. The Alliance, subsequently enlarged to include other political parties and renamed the National Front, has been ruling the country ever since.

The two eastern states of Sabah and Sarawak have a completely different historical background. Until the late nineteenth century, North Borneo (now Sabah) was part of the Sultanate of Brunei, but from 1881 it came under the management of the British North Borneo (Chartered) Company.[2] Like the countries in the region, North Borneo was under the

Japanese Occupation from 1942 to 1945, and thereafter it eventually became a Crown Colony under the British on 15 July 1946. Sarawak was also part of the Brunei Sultanate in the early years. On 24 September 1841, the Sultan declared James Brooke as the Rajah and governor of Sarawak. Rajah Brooke and his descendants continue to rule Sarawak, and after the Japanese Occupation Sir Wymer Brooke ceded Sarawak to Britain on 1 July 1946.[3]

The Federation of Malaya was expanded on 16 September 1963 with the formation of Malaysia notwithstanding the opposition from Indonesia and the Philippines. The larger political unit of Malaysia includes the eleven states in the former Federation of Malaya as well as the internally self-governing colony of Singapore and the two colonies of Sarawak and North Borneo (now Sabah). By participating in this new political development, the three colonies achieved their independence within Malaysia. The larger political partnership did not function smoothly, and, because of irreconcilable differences, the membership of Singapore in Malaysia came to an abrupt end on 9 August 1965 when it was forced to secede and thus became an independent country by itself. Since then Malaysia comprises the eleven states in Peninsular Malaysia and the two states of Sarawak and Sabah in the island of Borneo. Four states, Penang, Malacca, Sarawak and Sabah have an appointed Governor and a Chief Minister heading the elected state legislative council, while the other nine states have a hereditary Sultan and a Mentri Besar as head of the elected state legislature.

ECONOMY

Compared to the pre-independence period in the mid-1950s, the economy of Malaysia is now quite advanced and broadly based, with manufacturing accounting for about 32 per cent of the gross domestic product (GDP) and mining and quarrying some 15 per cent.[4] Wholesale and retail trade, and hotels and restaurants contributed 13 per cent to GDP and finance, insurance, real estate and business about 11 per cent. The contribution of the agricultural sector has been reduced to only 9 per cent. The prospect for further growth lies in the services sector such as finance, tourism and education.

During the colonial period, the economy was too dependent on rubber production and tin mining, which were subjected to frequent wide fluctuation in commodity prices and export earnings. Oil palm was one of the cash crops introduced as part of the agricultural diversification programme aimed at injecting greater stability in the economy. The cultivation of oil palm has proved to be quite successful, with the land area devoted to this crop standing at 4.05 hectares or two-thirds of the total cultivated area in the country.[5] About 60 per cent of the oil palm land are located in estates and the other 40 per cent in smallholdings. The cultivation of oil palm has grown to such an extent that Malaysia has became one of the major exporters of palm oil.

The expansion of oil palm was accompanied by a decline in rubber cultivation, falling to 1.24 million hectares or one-fifth of the total cultivated area. Only some 5 per cent of the land planted with rubber trees belong to estates and the other large 95 per cent to smallholdings.[6] The decline in rubber land in estates may be attributed to the fragmentation of some estates and the substitution of rubber with oil palm. The acreage devoted to rubber in smallholdings has also declined as the small farmers started to switch to oil palm with government assistance. However, Malaysia is still one of the largest rubber producers in the world.

Paddy cultivation on 0.68 million hectares, the traditional occupation of the rural folks, now occupies third position viewed in terms of cultivated area.[7] Paddy is grown entirely in small farms, located chiefly in the fertile low-lying plains of Perlis, Kedah, Kelantan and Trengganu. Strenuous efforts are being made by the government to increase the output of rice so as to raise the living standard of the predominantly Bumiputera paddy farmers. Some of the more notable measures are huge irrigation works, subsidised fertilizers, improved seedlings and better credit facilities. Such measures, coupled with double-cropping where possible and new paddy land converted from virgin jungle and swampland, have resulted in a marked rise in paddy production. Rice does not fetch any significant export earnings since almost all of the annual harvest is consumed within the country. What is significant is that the aim of self-sufficiency in rice has been almost achieved, with corresponding improvement in the living standard of the paddy farmers.

Coconut is one of the crops cultivated to meet local needs as well as foreign demand. Some 0.13 million hectares or 2.1 per cent of the total cultivated area are devoted to coconut cultivation, and almost all are situated in smallholdings.[8] A less important cash crop introduced to diversify the agricultural sector is cocoa, which is cultivated in some 33,000 hectares of land. The other crops with smaller acreage are pineapple, pepper, tobacco, tea, fruits and vegetables, usually grown by small farmers.

Another component of the economic strategy designed to broaden and strengthen the economy was the launching of an industrialisation programme to reduce the dependency on a few export earners and, more importantly, to provide jobs to the rapidly expanding labour force.[9] Among the more important measures taken by the government to promote industrialisation were the establishment of industrial estates with all the essential manufacturing facilities, the introduction of various forms of tax incentives, and the issue of liberal work permits to skilled foreigners required to manage the factories. The manufacturing activity is now quite broadly based, producing a wide range of light to heavy products. The importance of manufacturing is underlined by the 31 per cent it contributes to the gross domestic product.

For quite a long time, the mining industry was dominated by tin mining, with the mines operated and owned by Chinese entrepreneurs at the beginning and subsequently by British-owned companies utilising capital-intensive dredges to mine the tin.[10] The tin mines are located mainly along the western coastal belt of West Malaysia, especially in the Kinta valley in Perak and Klang valley in Selangor. As the other sectors of the economy expanded, the share of tin products in the total export earnings were reduced. Besides, oil and gas explorations in the offshore regions along the coastline began to be intensified, and oil discoveries and natural gas strikes were made. The petroleum industry under the management of the state-owned National Petroleum Board (Petronas) has overtaken tin mining and became a key player in the national economy of the country.

The development of the Malaysian economy was further transformed in recent years by the introduction of the New Economy Policy (NEP) in 1970. The new strategy, an outcome of the May 1969 race riots, was designed to eradicate poverty by raising the income level and increasing employment opportunities for all citizens, and thus correct economic imbalance so as to eliminate the identification of race with economic activity. The country has been experiencing an annual growth rate of some 5 to 9 per cent in recent years, attaining a per capita income of about US$4,930 in 2005. This compares favourably with the corresponding figure of US$2,665 for Thailand, US$1,368 for Indonesia, and US$1,071 for the Philippines, but less so with Singapore which has a per capita income of US$26,833.

DEMOGRAPHIC DATA

The taking of a census in Malaysia has its origins in the beginning of the nineteenth century when the inhabitants of the newly established Straits Settlements of Penang, Malacca and Singapore were first separately counted in 1801, 1828 and 1824 respectively. Thereafter, counts were made almost every year and later at longer intervals, and by 1836 eight were held in Penang, seven in Malacca and eleven in Singapore. The crude statistics of these counts were collected and published by T.J. Newbold.[11] After 1836 it appears that three further counts were conducted in the Straits Settlements in 1840, 1849 and 1960, and the results classified by sex and race were reproduced by T. Braddell in his book.[12] The statistics produced from these counts completed prior to 1871 were not only extremely narrow in scope but also seriously in error in many respects. Very limited demographic value can be placed on these early population statistics though they are of some historical interest.

The first proper census as understood in the modern form was conducted in the Straits Settlements in 1871 as part of the overall colonial census programme implemented throughout the British Empire.[13] In each of these settlements of Penang, Malacca and Singapore a committee of government officials was in charge of the census and each committee produced a report consisting of a brief administrative account and about twenty pages of basic tables. Another census in the same format was held in 1881 in the Straits Settlements. The year 1891 saw the Federated Malay States inaugurating the first proper census and the Straits Settlements conducting the third one under, not committees, but a single superintendent of census. A decade later similar censuses were held in the Straits Settlements and in the Federated Malay States. The year 1911 was of special significance in that it witnessed not only the continuation of the decennial censuses in these two regions, but also the launching of census taking in the Unfederated Malay States. Population statistics for the whole territory now known as Peninsular Malaysia were thus made available for the first time in 1911. This delay in the availability of population statistics for the whole of the peninsula may be attributed to the varying degrees of British influence and hence the different systems of government among the various parts of the country.

In 1921 a population census for the combined territory of Peninsular Malaysia and Singapore was undertaken by a single superintendent who was also responsible for bringing out the census report. The next decennial census was conducted on the same scale in 1931. A census was planned for April 1941 but the increasing difficulties arising from the imminence of war led to the abandonment of the project and to a break in the long series of decennial censuses. After the war plans were immediately drawn up to enumerate the population and a common census for the whole of Peninsular Malaysia and Singapore was finally completed in 1947. The next postwar census taken in 1957 was a departure from the three previous ones in that Peninsular Malaysia, being a distinct political unit at that time, was separately enumerated under one single superintendent.

With the formation of Malaysia in 1963, the next census was held in 1970 on a pan-Malaysia basis, covering the eleven states in West Malaysia and the two states in East Malaysia.[14] A census of housing was incorporated in the population census, and hence the expanded census conducted in 1970 was known as a Population and Housing Census. The scope of the census in regard to population was quite comprehensive, with the usual topics in the previous censuses supplemented by new topics deemed useful for natural socio-economic planning.

The second pan-Malaysia census of Population was held ten years later in 1980 with 10 June 1980 as the census date. In the main, the method of conducting this census was essentially similar to that used in the previous census.[15] As for the topics included, Table 1.1 shows that one old topic on number of years married was dropped, and three new topics were introduced. They are age at first marriage, place of previous residence, and reason for migration. Another change was the presentation of the census data for an additional geographic unit carved out of Selangor to form the Federal territory of Kuala Lumpur in 1974. The census results were published in the form of two general reports covering the whole of Malaysia and thirteen separate reports for the thirteen states.

The third Population Census of Malaysia was held in 1991 instead of 1990, thus breaking the usual ten-year interval for conducting a census as recommended by the United Nations.[16] The census was held much later in the year, viz. 14 August, instead of near the middle of the year. Another departure from previous censuses was the drastic change in the scope of the census. Whilst only two new topics were introduced, no less than fifteen previous topics were omitted as can be observed in Table 1.1. The sharp reduction in the number of topics has obviously made it impossible to analyse the affected data on a continuous time series basis.

TABLE 1.1

Topics Covered in the Population and Housing Censuses of Four Pan-Malaysia Censuses, 1970–2000

Census Topics	1970	1980	1991	2000
Geographic Characteristics				
Place where person was found on Census Day	√	√	√	X
Place of usual residence at time of Census	X	X	√	√
Demographic and Social Characteristics				
Sex	√	√	√	√
Age	√	√	√	√
Date of Birth	√	√	√	√
Marital Status	√	√	√	√
Ethnicity	√	√	√	√
Religion	√	√	√	√
Citizenship/residence status	√	√	√	√
Identity card colour	√	√	X	X
Language spoken	√	√	X	X
Disability	√	√	X	√
Fertility and Mortality				
Number of children born alive	√	√	X	√
Number of children living	√	√	X	√
Age at first marriage	X	√	X	X
Number of times married	√	√	X	X
Numbers of years married	√	X	X	X
Migration Characteristics				
Birthplace	√	√	√	√
Period of residence in Malaysia	√	√	X	X
Period of residence in present locality	√	√	X	X
Place of last previous residence	X	√	X	X
Reason for migration	X	√	X	X
Place of residence five years ago	X	X	√	√
Year of first arrival in Malaysia	X	X	X	√
Education Characteristics				
Literacy	√	√	X	√
School attendance	√	√	√	√
Highest level of schooling attained	√	√	√	√
Highest educational certificate obtained	√	√	√	√
Vocational training	√	√	X	X
Field of study	X	X	X	√
Place of obtaining certificate/diploma/degree	X	X	X	√
Economic Characteristics				
Type of economic activity (during previous week)	√	√	√	√
Number of hours worked (during previous week)	X	X	√	√
Type of economic activity (during last twelve months)	√	√	X	X
Occupation	√	√	√	√
Industry	√	√	√	√
Employment status	√	√	√	√
Occupation sector (government/private/individual)	X	X	X	√

The census results were published in the same manner as before, two general reports and thirteen state reports. However, separate figures are made available for the new federal territory of Labuan, converted in 1984 from the district of Labuan in the state of Sabah, and of course for the earlier federal territory of Kuala Lumpur.

The latest Census of Population was held nine years later in 2000 with 5 July as the census date.[17] In contrast to the large reduction in the number of topics in the last census, the 2000 Census reinstated eight topics previously dropped, and only one old topic on place where person was found on census days was omitted. More information is therefore available from the latest census, though time-series for the reinstated topics have been broken. Indeed, the frequent changes in the number of topics in the four pan-Malaysia censuses shown in Table 1.1 make it rather problematic to examine certain characteristics of the population for the whole thirty-year period. A radical departure from the three previous censuses was the release of the results in one general report and several reports on subject basis. No state reports for the thirteen states were published.

The other sources of statistics used in our study of the population of Malaysia are the well-established system of registering births and deaths and the annual survey of labour force started in the 1970s. Compulsory registration of births and deaths were first introduced in 1872 in Penang and Malacca, followed by the other states in later years. It was only in 1934 that the whole of West Malaysia, and many years later in Sabah and Sarawak, that birth and death registration became compulsory. Although the Registrar-General of Births and Death is responsible for the registration of births and deaths,[18] the vital statistics derived from this system are processed and published by the Department of Statistics. This department is also responsible for conducting the annual labour force survey, and the statistics are published by the department in an annual report.[19]

ADMINISTRATIVE DIVISION

The operation of a population census in a country is normally executed at the various administrative levels; the census statistics for some topics are published according to small geographical units. In Malaysia, the whole country has been divided into 13 states, 11 in Peninsular Malaysia and 2 in East Malaysia. In addition, there are two smaller areas designated as federal territories, Kuala Lumpur and Labuan. Kuala Lumpur, with a population of 1.38 million, was formerly part of Selangor; it is the seat of the Federal Government and centre for business. Labuan, with a tiny population of 76,100, was converted into a federal territory from the former district of Labuan in Sabah. In our study at state level, we have decided to treat Labuan as part of Sabah rather than a separate entity since this arrangement will have an extremely negligible effect on the regional analysis of the population. On account of its importance viewed in terms of population, commercial activity and administrative function, Kuala Lumpur will be treated as a separate unit rather than merged with Selangor state.

Each of the states in Peninsular Malaysia, except Kelantan, is divided into districts, and each district is sub-divided into mukims. The administration of each district is under a District Officer and each mukim is under the charge of a Penghulu. In Kelantan the administrative district is known as *jajahan*, divided into *daerahs* and further divided into mukims. The state of Sabah is divided into administrative districts, but each of these districts has not been sub-divided into smaller units. The other eastern state of Sarawak is divided into 9 divisions, which are sub-divided into administrative districts. There are no mukims in these two states.

Because of its small size, Perlis has not been subdivided into administrative districts. Similarly, Kuala Lumpur and Labuan are special cases and have not been divided into administrative districts. At the time of the population census in 2000, there were 134 administrative districts, in addition to the 2 federal territories. Some of the statistics collected in the population censuses are presented at the district level, and in rare cases even at the mukim level.

Notes

1. C. Mary Turnbull, *A History of Malaysia, Singapore and Brunei* (London: Allen & Unwin, 1989).
2. S. Ranjit, *The Making of Sabah, 1865–1941* (University of Malaya Press, 2000).
3. Vernon L. Porrith, *British Colonial Rule in Sarawak, 1946–1963* (Kuala Lumpur: Oxford University Press, 1997).
4. Malaysia, *Yearbook of Statistics Malaysia 2006* (Kuala Lumpur: Department of Statistics, 2006).
5. Malaysia, *Monthly Statistical Bulletin, June 2006* (Kuala Lumpur: Department of Statistics, 2006).

6. Malaysia, *Rubber Statistics Handbook, 2005* (Kuala Lumpur: Department of Statistics, 2006).
7. Malaysia, *Yearbook of Statistics Malaysia 2006* (Kuala Lumpur: Department of Statistics, 2006 .
8. Ibid.
9. Babara Watson Andaya and Leonard Y. Andaya, *A History of Malaysia* (Honolulu: University of Hawaii Press, 2001).
10. Wong Lin Ken, *The Malayan Tin Industry up to 1914* (Tucson: University of Arizona, 1965).
11. T.J. Newbold, *Political and Statistical Account of the British Settlement in the Straits of Malacca*, Vol. 1 (London: John Murray, 1939).
12. T. Braddell, *Statistics of the British Possessions in the Straits of Malacca* (Pinang: Pinang Gazette Printing Office, 1861).
13. Saw Swee-Hock, "Appendiex D: Sources of Demographic Statistics" in *The Population of Peninsular Malaysia* (Kuala Lumpur: Singapore University Press, 1988).
14. R. Chander, *1970 General Report of the Population Census of Malaysia*, Volume 1 (Kuala Lumpur: Department of Statistics, 1977).
15. Khoo Teik Huat, *1980 General Report of the Population Census*, Volume 1 (Kuala Lumpur: Department of Statistics, 1983).
16. Khoo Soo Gim, *1991 General Report of the Population Census*, Volume 1 (Kuala Lumpur: Department of Statistics, 1995).
17. Haji Aziz bin Othman, *2000 General Report of the Population and Housing Census* (Kuala Lumpur: Department of Statistics, 2005).
18. Malaysia, *Vital Statistics, Malaysia*, for the years 1970 to 2003 (Kuala Lumpur: Department of Statistics).
19. Malaysia, *Labour Force Survey*, for the years 1970 to 2004 (Kuala Lumpur: Department of Statistics).

2

Population Growth and Distribution

In interpreting the figures in respect of population size and growth, we should be mindful of the population censuses not being conducted on a uniform time interval of ten years as practised in most countries. The holding of the third pan-Malaysia Census in 1991 has resulted in a break in the intercensal time interval, 10 years for the 1970–1980 period, 11 years for the 1980–1991 period and nine years for the 1991–2000 period. What this implies is that we should pay more attention to the figures for annual rate of growth rather than intercensal rate of growth presented in Table 2.1 and other tables where time-series data are included for the purpose of examining population trends.

It is also necessary to explain the presentation of the figures according to geographic areas. The practice of examining some of the census results in terms of three broad geographic regions in the census reports has been adopted in our analysis. West Malaysia, also known as Peninsular Malaysia, consists of eleven states and the Federal Territory of Kuala Lumpur with common land boundaries and shared historical, political and economic background. The two states of Sabah and Sarawak, collectively known as East Malaysia, are separated by the vast expense of the South China Sea, apart from their separate history, economy and population.

OVERALL POPULATION GROWTH

The figures for 1960 are obtained from the pre-Malaysia Censuses conducted in this year in Sabah[1] and Sarawak[2] and from intercensal population estimate for West Malaysia where the census was held in

1957 instead of 1950.[3] The changes in the size of the population over time are caused by natural increase and net international migration. The population of Malaysia prior to its establishment was estimated to total about 8,035,600 in the pre-merger year of 1960. By the first pan-Malaysia Census held in 1970 the population has grown to above the ten-million mark of 10,439,400, an increase of 2,405,800 or an annual growth rate of 2.7 per cent during this ten-year period.[4] In the second pan-Malaysia Census conducted in 1980 the population was enumerated as 13,136,100, an increase of 2,696,700 since 1970 or an annual growth rate of 2.3 per cent.[5] The race riots that flared up on 13 May 1969 in Kuala Lumpur started a fresh movement of non-Bumiputera persons outward to Singapore and other countries.

TABLE 2.1
Population Growth, 1960–2005

Year	Population ('000)	Increase ('000)	Annual Growth Rate
1960	8,035.6	—	—
1970	10,439.4	2,403.8	2.7
1980	13,136.1	2,696.7	2.3
1991	17,563.4	4,427.3	2.7
2000	23,274.7	5,711.3	3.1
2005	26,127.7	2,853.0	2.3

Thereafter, the population increase recovered during the eleven-year period to bring it to 17,563,400 in 1991, giving an annual growth rate of 2.7 per cent.[6] The latest Census held in 2000 reveals that the population had passed the twenty-million mark with a figure of 23,274,700.[7] This represents a large increase of 5,711,300 over that enumerated nine years ago in 1991, with the annual growth rate accelerated further to 3.1 per cent. This high growth rate can only come about with the substained large inflow of international migration, consisting primarily of migrant labour to elevate the labour shortage in certain sectors of the economy. The latest postcensal estimate for the year 2005 gives a figure of 26,127,700, an increase of 2,853,000 or 2.3 per cent per year during the five-year period 2000–2005. The slackening growth rate may be attributed to the repatriation of foreign workers, particularly illegal Indonesian workers.

During the intercensal period 1970–1980, the population increase amounted to 2,696,700 but natural increase was 3,036,200, giving a net migration of 339,500 outward bound. At that time there was only a small inflow of migrant workers but a large outflow of particularly Chinese to Singapore and other countries following the race riots in 1969.[8] The next intercensal period 1980–1991 recorded a much smaller negative net migration of 52,900, resulting from a population increase of 4,427,300 and a natural increase of 4,479,800. A dramatic turn occurred during the period 1991–2000 when the population increase was 5,711,300, with natural increase contributing 3,903,200 or 68.3 per cent and migration 1,808,700 or 31.7 per cent. The significant role played by migration in the population growth of the country was caused mainly by the inflow of legal and illegal migrant workers as the shortage of labour became increasing acute during the high economic growth in the nineties.

The population increase during the postcensal period 2000–2005 came to 2,853,000, with 2,139,900 or 75.0 per cent contributed by natural increase and the other 713,100 or 25.0 per cent by migration. As observed earlier, during this five-year period the annual rate of population growth had slackened to 2.3 per cent. In early May 2004, the Malaysian government started to talk about tightening existing rulers and procedures governing the hiring of foreign workers due to an oversupply of migrant workers. The Minister for Human Resources, Fong Choon Onn, said that Malaysia needed about one million foreign workers but there were some 1.2 million registered with his Ministry, not forgetting the illegal immigrants who do not bother to register.[9] Some 84 per cent of the foreign workers were from Indonesia, while the rest came from the Philippines, Thailand and South Asia.

Before the end of 2004 Malaysia had begun to take steps to repatriate the illegal migrant workers back to particularly Indonesia. In October 2004 the Malaysian government offered a four-month amnesty to the estimated one-million illegal immigrants, about 0.8 million Indonesians, to return to their country during the Muslim fasting month without being prosecuted.[10] At the expiry of the amnesty in end-February 2005, about 392,000 had left Malaysia, the majority under the amnesty programme and a small group forcefully repatriated. The huge exodus of foreign workers has led to factories and plantations reeling over a severe shortage of cheap foreign labour. Since very few of the illegals who left were prepared to return on a legal basis, Malaysia was forced to recruit foreign workers from other countries such as Vietnam, Myanmar, Philippines, Thailand and the South Asian countries.[11]

REGIONAL POPULATION GROWTH

Some interesting differences in the pattern of population growth among the three regions are underlined by the figures shown in Table 2.2. Between 1960 and 2005, the population of Sarawak grew steadily at the moderate level of 2.2 to 2.8 per cent per annum. This fairly stable growth rate may be attributed to natural increase, not subjected to violent fluctuations constituting the principal factor of population growth in this eastern state.[12] The inward flow of international migration as well as internal migration from the other states in Malaysia have always been insignificant as compared to the other two regions. During the whole forty-five years, the population was enlarged by slightly more than three-fold, rising from 744,500 to 2,312,600 in 2005.

TABLE 2.2
Population Growth by Region, 1960–2005

Year	Population ('000)	Increase ('000)	Annual Growth Rate
	West Malaysia		
1960	6,836.7	—	—
1970	8,809.6	1,972.9	2.6
1980	11,426.6	2,617.0	2.7
1991	14,131.7	2,705.1	2.0
2000	18,523.6	5,880.6	4.3
2005	20,883.4	2,359.8	2.4
	Sabah		
1960	454.4	—	—
1970	653.6	199.2	3.7
1980	955.7	302.1	3.9
1991	1,788.9	833.2	5.9
2000	2,679.6	890.7	4.5
2005	3,015.2	335.6	2.3
	Sarawak		
1960	744.5	—	—
1970	976.3	231.8	2.8
1980	1,235.6	259.3	2.4
1991	1,642.8	407.2	2.7
2000	2,071.5	428.7	2.3
2005	2,312.6	241.1	2.2

A completely different pattern of population growth was experienced in Sabah, including the tiny Federal Territory of Labuan in all the tables under discussion. It is more convenient for us to adopt this procedure in our analysis, more so when the merging of this minute population with the far larger population of Sabah would not in any way affect the salient features of the various aspects of the latter population. In 2000 the population of Labuan was only 76,067 as against the huge population of 2,603,485 in Sabah.

A consistently higher rate of population growth was recorded in Sabah. The population increased by a higher rate of 3.7 per cent during the intercensal period 1960–1970, and accelerated to 3.9 per cent and 5.9 per cent during the next two periods. A slight slackening to 4.5 per cent was recorded during the period 1991–2000, but dropped sharply to 2.3 per cent during 2000–2005. The exceptionally rapid rate of population growth during the major period under consideration was due to the fairly high volume of natural increase and, more importantly, to the sustained large inflow of labour migrants from Indonesia and the Philippines. The population of Sabah was enlarged by about 6.5 times, shooting up to 2,931,700 in 2005 from the low of only 454,400 in 1960. In fact, by 1991 the population of Sabah had overtaken that of Sarawak, and has remained so since then.

In the larger region of West Malaysia, the population was estimated to total 6,836,700 in 1960. By the first pan-Malaysia Census held in 1970, the population had reached 8,809,600, representing an annual growth rate of 2.6 per cent. This rate of population increase was raised slightly to 2.7 per cent in the next intercensal period 1970–1980, followed by a downturn to 2.0 per cent during the period 1980–1991. Subsequently, this rate of population increase accelerated to 4.3 per cent during the next period 1991–2000, but was reduced to only 2.4 per cent during the latest period 2000–2005. The total population was enlarged to 20,883,400, 3.1 times larger than the figure of 6,836,700 in 1960. The inward flow of international migration, from particularly Indonesia, was responsible for the high rate of population increase in West Malaysia. Many of the newcomers were illegal migrant labourers and were repatriated back to their country recently, and hence the lower growth rate recorded during 2000–2005.

An idea of the different rate of population growth in the different parts of West Malaysia may be obtained in Table 2.3 showing the annual rate of population increase since the first pan-Malaysia Census held in

TABLE 2.3
Annual Rate of Population Growth in
West Malaysian States, 1970–2005

State	1970–1980	1980–1991	1991–2000	2000–2005
Johore	2.1	2.5	2.6	2.5
Kedah	1.2	1.7	2.1	3.5
Kelantan	2.3	2.9	0.9	2.8
Malacca	1.0	1.1	2.0	2.3
Negri Sembilan	1.4	2.1	1.9	2.0
Penang	1.5	1.5	1.8	2.3
Pahang	4.2	2.8	1.9	2.1
Perak	1.1	0.7	0.4	2.0
Perlis	1.8	2.2	0.8	1.9
Selangor	3.7	4.3	6.1	2.5
Trengganu	2.6	3.4	1.2	2.5
Kuala Lumpur	3.5	2.0	1.3	2.4

1970. Over the years most states do not appear to exhibit any clear trend, bearing in mind that the growth rate in each state would depend on births, deaths, net internal migration from other states, and net external migration from other countries. Selangor experienced the highest and fastest annual growth during the first three decades, accelerating from 3.7 per cent during 1970–80 to 6.1 per cent during 1991–2000. This is connected to the slower growth recorded in the enclosed Federal Territory of Kuala Lumpur, being lowered from 2.6 per cent to 1.2 per cent during the same time. As the centre of business and government, Kuala Lumpur has been the magnet for locals and foreigners seeking work, but many were compelled to reside in cheaper and less crowded accommodation across its borders with Selangor.

Three other states, Johore, Penang and Kedah, recorded an upward trend in their annual growth but at a much slower acceleration over the years. Johore had benefited from the inflow of foreign workers in the agricultural sector and Penang by foreigners and persons from neighbouring states to work in the manufacturing sector. Kedah on the other hand, received some inflow of persons fleeing from the unsettled conflict in southern Thailand.

The reverse trend was experienced by Pahang where the annual growth rate slackened from 4.2 per cent during 1970–1980 to 1.9 per cent during 1991–2000. This may be attributed to outward migration to other parts of the country. The other state exhibiting a slackening in the annual growth was Perak, with the rate being reduced from 1.1 per cent to 0.4 per cent. No definite trend is discernable in the remaining states. Looking at the latest period 2000–2005, the highest growth rate was registered by Kedah with 3.5 per cent, followed by Kelantan with 2.8 per cent. The recent upheavals between the predominantly Muslim population and the Thai authorities have resulted in the southward move of people from southern Thailand into the two northern states.

URBAN/RURAL POPULATION GROWTH

It is useful to examine the growth of the population separately in the urban and rural areas in Malaysia with a very large rural sector. The definition of an urban area varies from one country to another, and even within a particular country changes in the definition may be introduced in the population censuses. In the early censuses conducted in Malaysia, urban areas have been equated to gazetted administrative districts with a population of 1,000 or more inhabitants. The process of gazetting an area is an essential part of government administration involving the careful mapping of the area to establish the boundaries which are then notified in the government gazette for public information. The old definition is now considered as too restrictive, and the more realistic definition of an urban area with 10,000 or more inhabitants is now used.[13] It is more important to note that this definition has also been employed in the other sections of this chapter dealing with urban-rural classification. Another important point to bear in mind is the availability of data for urban and rural areas from census years only, and hence the estimated figures for 2005 are not available.

The growth of the population in the urban or rural area is determined by not only natural increase and international migration, but internal movement of people within the country. The first intercensal period 1970–1980 witnessed a jump in the urban population from 2,798,600 to 4,492,400, representing an increase of 6.3 per cent. This growth rate accelerated to 98.2 per cent during 1980–1991, but slowed down to 62.1 per cent during the most recent period. In sharp contrast, the annual growth rate recorded in the rural area managed to reach only 13.1 per cent, 0.2 per cent and 21.1 per cent during these three respective intercensal periods. The extremely rapid increase in the urban population

TABLE 2.4
Population Growth by Urban/Rural Area, 1970–2000

Year	Population ('000)	Intercensal Increase	
		Number ('000)	Percentage
		Urban	
1970	2,793.6	—	—
1980	4,492.4	1,693.8	60.5
1991	8,893.6	4,406.2	98.1
2000	14,426.9	5,528.3	62.1
		Rural	
1970	7,640.8	—	—
1980	8,643.7	1,002.9	13.1
1991	8,664.8	21.1	0.2
2000	8,847.8	183.0	21.1

in all these years car be traced primary to the movement of people from the rural sector to the urban conurbation and partly to the relocation of small town dwellers to the bigger towns.[14]

It should be mentioned that the larger increase in the urban population recorded during 1980–1991 may be partly due to the adoption of a new definition of urban areas in the 1991 Census.[15] Prior to this census the definition was confined solely to gazetted areas with a population of at least 10,000 within the administrative boundaries. In the 1991 Census the definition of urban centres was extended to include areas having urban characteristics around the periphery of the boundaries of the gazetted town. In general, urban centres were therefore defined as gazetted areas and their adjoining built-up areas with a combined population of 10,000 persons or more. The new definition, also adopted in the 2000 Census, was deemed to be a more realistic measure of the level of urbanisation.

REGIONAL POPULATION DISTRIBUTION

The distribution of the population over the various parts of Malaysia can be traced to the historical and economic development of the country. In the early days, prior to the incursion of European powers, the people lived in the settlements sprung along the coasts and riverine banks where they engaged in fishing and farming. Except for Sabah and Sarawak, the densely forested interior was almost devoid of inhabitants. Towards the middle of the nineteenth century, the distribution of the population began to undergo some changes consequent on the development of tin mining in Perak, Selangor and Negri Sembilan by Chinese immigrant settlers. At that time, there was also some clustering of the population in gambier, pepper, tapioca, sugar and coffee plantations.[16]

At the end of the nineteenth century, another important event affecting population distribution was the introduction of rubber as a plantation crop with the help of cheap immigrant labour from south India. The rubber plantations sprang up in the western foothills of the Peninsula with well-drained terrain and near existing railway lines to transport the rubber to the seaports for export to the industrialised countries in the west. The deep-water harbours are sheltered from the southwest monsoon by Sumatra and from the northeast monsoon by the central mountain range. For more recent years, the population was drawn towards industrial estates located near or in the urban centres in usually the western side of the country. As mentioned earlier, there was also the movement of people into the urban centres where economic activities are most vibrant.

The continuous development of the country along the western part of the country would naturally be reflected in the geographic distribution of the population. Obviously, each of the 13 states has never been populated in proportion to the size of the land area since land size is only one of the many factors determining population distribution. The distribution of land area and population according to the estimates for 2005 is presented in Table 2.5. Malaysia has a total land area of 329,847 square kilometres, with 39.9 per cent in West Malaysia, 37.7 per cent in Sarawak, and 22.4 per cent in Sabah. However, almost 79.6 per cent of the total population of 26,127,700 in 2005 was to be found in West Malaysia, while only 11.5 per cent and 8.9 per cent were residing in Sabah and Sarawak respectively. Sarawak stands out as the typical example of little relationship between land size and population since it has the largest land area but the lowest population density of only 17 persons per square kilometre. The figures seem to suggest there is some inverse relationship between land area and population.

The Federal Territory of Kuala Lumpur with the smallest land area has the highest population density of 6,404 persons per square kilometre.

TABLE 2.5

Population Distribution and Density by Region and State, 2005

Region/State	Area in square kilometre	Population ('000)	Population per square kilometre
Region			
MALAYSIA	329,847	26,127.7	79
West Malaysia	131,598	20,799.9	158
Sabah	73,711	3,015.2	41
Sarawak	124,450	2,312.6	19
West Malayan State			
Johore	18,987	3,101.2	163
Kedah	9,425	1,848.1	196
Kelantan	15,024	1,505.6	100
Malacca	1,652	713.0	432
Negri Sembilan	6,644	946.3	142
Pahang	35,965	1,427.0	40
Penang	1,031	1,468.8	1,425
Perak	21,005	2,256.4	107
Perlis	795	224.5	282
Selangor	7,960	4,736.1	595
Trengganu	12,955	1,016.5	78
Kuala Lumpur	243	1,556.2	6,404

This high density is to be expected since Kuala Lumpur is the premier city with almost no rural area to speak off. Among the 13 states, Penang with the second largest city has the highest density of 1,425 persons per square kilometre, followed by Selangor with a much lower figure of 595 persons. Fairly high density can be observed in Malacca with 432 persons and Perlis with 282 persons. At the slightly lower level are Kedah with 196 persons, Johor with 163 persons and Negri Sembilan with 142 persons. The lowest population density is situated in the eastern states of Kelantan with 100 persons, Trengganu with 78 persons, and Pahang with only 40 persons.

STATE RANKING BY POPULATION SIZE

Another way of looking at the distribution of the population is to examine the figures for the proportionate distribution of the population among the thirteen states and the Federal Territory of Kuala Lumpur provided in Table 2.6. Over the years a gradual shift in the proportionate distribution of the population among these states has taken place consequent on the different growth rate. Some states had experienced higher birth rates and lower death rates, some managed to attract more in-migrants than out-migrants, and still others had received a larger volume of immigrants from overseas. During the period 1970–2005, a diminution in their individual share of the total population was noticeable in six states. They are Penang falling from 7.4 per cent to 5.6 per cent, Perak from 15.0 to 8.6 per cent, Kedah from 9.1 to 7.1 per cent, Negri Sembilan from 4.6 to 3.6 per cent, Malacca from 3.9 to 2.7 per cent, and finally Perlis from 1.2 to 0.9 per cent.

Selangor stands out as the only state experiencing a clear gain in the share of the total population, being raised from 9.4 per cent to 18.1 per cent during the period. It has certainly benefited from the rapid development of Kuala Lumpur, resulting in the spillover of residents across the state boundary surrounding the Federal Territory. The vast expansion of the economy along the Klang valley, with the state capital

TABLE 2.6
Percentage Distribution of Population by State, 1970–2005

State	1970	1980	1991	2000	2005
Johore	12.2	12.0	11.8	11.8	11.9
Kedah	9.1	8.2	7.4	7.1	7.1
Kelantan	6.6	6.5	6.7	5.6	5.8
Malacca	3.9	3.4	2.9	2.7	2.7
Negri Sembilan	4.6	4.2	3.9	3.7	3.6
Pahang	4.8	5.8	5.9	5.5	5.5
Penang	7.4	6.9	6.1	5.6	5.6
Perak	15.0	13.3	10.7	8.8	8.6
Perlis	1.2	1.1	1.0	0.9	0.9
Sabah	6.3	7.3	10.2	11.3	11.2
Sarawak	9.4	9.4	9.4	9.9	8.9
Selangor	9.4	10.9	13.1	18.0	18.1
Trengganu	3.9	4.0	4.4	3.9	3.9
Kuala Lumpur	6.2	7.0	6.5	5.9	6.7
Total	100.0	100.0	100.0	100.0	100.0

of Shah Alam and Petaling Jaya, attracted settlers from every part of the country and also foreign workers. No clear uptrend or downtrend in their share of the total population appears to exist among the other five states. To a limited extent, the changes in the state proportion of the population would be reflected in a shift in the relative importance of the states, for example in terms of votes during election time.

A convenient method of illustrating the relative position of the thirteen states over the years is to present the ranking at the various years in the form of a diagram shown in Figure 2.1. It is apparent that Sabah has undergone the greatest improvement, moving up quickly from eighth place in 1970 to third in 2005. Another state that has shown an improvement, but by only two notches was Selangor, going up from third to first position. Interestingly, few states did not witness any

FIGURE 2.1
Changing Rank Order of States, 1970–2005

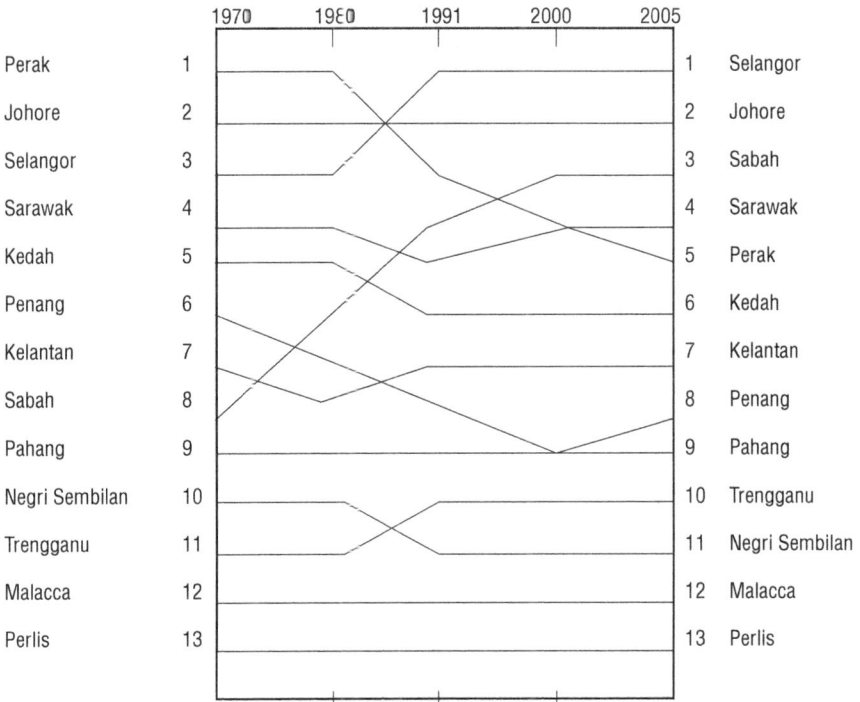

1970	1980	1991	2000	2005

Perak	1	1	Selangor
Johore	2	2	Johore
Selangor	3	3	Sabah
Sarawak	4	4	Sarawak
Kedah	5	5	Perak
Penang	6	6	Kedah
Kelantan	7	7	Kelantan
Sabah	8	8	Penang
Pahang	9	9	Pahang
Negri Sembilan	10	10	Trengganu
Trengganu	11	11	Negri Sembilan
Malacca	12	12	Malacca
Perlis	13	13	Perlis

change at all during the last thirty-five years, Johore remaining as
second, Pahang as ninth, Malacca as twelfth and Perlis as thirteenth.
Only two states were subjected to a pronounced worsening of their
relative position, Perak dropping steeply from first to fifth and Penang
from sixth to eighth. There are of course economic and political
significance underlying the shift in the relative size of the population
among the thirteen states.

URBAN/RURAL POPULATION DISTRIBUTION

Another aspect of population distribution that will be examined refers to
the changes in the population according to urban-rural classification
resulting from rapid urbanisation mentioned earlier.[17] In 1970 the
population residing in the urban centres numbered some 2,798,600 or
26.8 per cent as against the 7,640,800 or 73.2 per cent in the rural area.
Since then, there occurred a pronounced shift in the population between
the two areas, with the respective proportions moving towards 34.2 per
cent and 65.8 per cent in 1980 and 50.7 per cent and 49.8 per cent in
1991. By the time of the latest census conducted in 2000, the population
living in the urban area had swelled to 14,426,900 or 62.0 per cent, while
the number in the rural areas stood at 8,847,800 or 38.6 per cent. This
urbanisation trend, a common worldwide phenomenon, has been exerting

TABLE 2.7
Distribution of Population by
Urban/Rural Area, 1970–2000

Year	Urban	Rural	Total
	Number		
1970	2,798.6	7,640.8	10,439.4
1980	4,492.6	8,643.7	13,136.1
1991	8,898.6	8,664.8	17,563.4
2000	14,426.9	8,847.8	23,274.4
	Percentage		
1970	26.8	73.2	100.0
1980	34.2	65.8	100.0
1991	50.7	49.3	100.0
2000	62.0	38.0	100.0

intense pressures in the urban conurbations with regard to meeting the essential needs of the residents, particularly jobs and housing.

The proportion of urban population as derived from the 2000 census varies greatly among the thirteen states. As to be expected, the proportion of urban population in Kuala Lumpur was 100 per cent, followed closely by Selangor with 87.6 per cent and Penang with 80.1 per cent. Malacca and Johore have almost the same proportion, 67.2 per cent and 65.2 per cent respectively. The least urban states are situated in the north part of the country, 34.2 per cent in Kelantan, 34.3 per cent in Perlis and 39.3 in Kedah.

An interesting aspect of urban population) concerns the distribution of the population according to the size of the urban centres. This is shown in Table 2.8 providing the urban centres and their population in terms of five class sizes from the minimum of 10,000 persons upwards. Between 1980 and 1991, there was almost a doubling of the number of urban centres as well as their population. The number of urban centres increased by 92.5 per cent from 67 in 1980 to 129 in 1991, while the population was enlarged by 98.1 per cent from 4,492,400 to 8,898,600 during the same period. The increase was less remarkable during the latest period 1991–2000 when the number of urban centres went up by only 31.8 to reach 170 in 2000 and the population by 54.1 per cent to reach 13,714,800. The differences in the growth of urban centres and their population between the two intercensal periods may be attributed to the broadening of the definition of urban centres from the 1991 Census onwards.

TABLE 2.8
Distribution of Urban Centres and Population
by Class Size, 1980–2000

Class Size	Urban Centres			Population ('000)		
	1980	1991	2000	1980	1991	2000
150,000 & Over	8	15	27	2,456.1	4,799.4	8,912.1
75,000 – 149,999	6	15	13	663.2	1,665.5	1,373.5
50,000 – 74,999	8	9	14	500.7	538.0	825.7
25,000 – 49,999	9	23	36	321.0	810.0	1,281.4
10,000 – 24,999	36	67	80	553.4	1,085.8	1,321.9
Total	67	129	170	4,492.4	8,898.6	13,714.8

The distribution of the population according to the classification used in the table is quite skewed as indicated by the 54.7 per cent in the upperment class of at least 150,000 persons in 1980. This proportion remained essentially the same, 53.2 per cent, eleven years later in 1991, but was enhanced to 65.0 per cent in 2000. Urbanisation has undoubtedly gathered pace in recent years, not forgetting the entry of foreign workers in the large urban centres.

When the definition of urban centres was expanded in 1991, the population in the smallest class of 10,000–24,999 was expanded by 98.0 per cent during the period 1980–1991. But this expansion managed to attain 54.1 per cent only during the latest intercensal period. Over the years some of the urban centres have moved up by one class size as the number of persons residing in the various centres increased an account of natural increase, internal movement from rural and urban areas, and new foreigners choosing to stay in these urban centres.

Out of the total population of 14,426,900 enumerated in the 170 urban centres with at least 10,000 inhabitants in 2000, some 7,733,600 or 53.6 per cent were residing in top twenty urban centres.[18] The highlights of these twenty large urban centres and their respective population size are shown in Table 2.9. Not surprisingly, the Federal Territory of Kuala Lumpur has remained the premier city with a huge population size of 1,305,800. This was twice the size of the next largest urban centre, Johore Bahru with 642,900, which has in fact moved up from its previous third position in 1991. Apart from Kuala Lumpur, the six urban centres of Klang, Subang Jaya, Petaling Jaya, Ampang Jaya, Shah Alam and Kajang in the top twenty confirm the dominance of Selangor as the principal place for both locals and foreigners to benefit from the vibrant economy in this premier state.

A comparison of the two sets of census figures will disclose that six urban centres in the top twenty list in 2000 have registered an improvement in this ranking since 1991. Moreover, three urban centres, Petaling Jaya, Ampang Jaya and Kajang, appeared for the first time in the top twenty list. The radical shifts in the ranking of urban centres since 1991 may be attributed to the rapid, though unbalanced, development among the different parts of the country. The other interesting feature refers to the no-appearance of all the state capitals in the top twenty list. Only nine of the thirteen capitals managed to appear in this list, a reflection again of the uneven socio-economic development prevailing among the various states. The need for a more balanced regional

TABLE 2.9
Population in Top Urban Centres, 1991 and 2000

Urban Centre	2000		1991	
	Ranking	Number ('000)	Ranking	Number ('000)
Kuala Lumpur	1	1,305.8	1	1,145.3
Johore Bahru (sc)	2	642.9	3	468.8
Klang	3	626.7	4	368.4
Ipoh (sc)	4	536.8	2	468.8
Subang Jaya	5	437.1		
Petaling Jaya	6	432.6	5	351.0
Kuching (sc)	7	422.9	6	277.9
Ampang Jaya	8	357.9	18	148.4
Shah Alam (sc)	9	314.4		
Kota Kinabalu (sc)	10	306.9	14	160.2
Seremban (sc)	11	290.7	11	193.2
Kuantan (sc)	12	288.7	10	202.4
Sandakan	13	276.8	15	156.7
Kuala Trengganu (sc)	14	255.5	8	228.1
Kota Bahru (sc)	15	251.8	7	234.6
Tawau	16	213.7	19	124.9
Kajang	17	205.7		
Taiping	18	199.3	12	186.9
Alor Star (sc)	19	186.4	13	164.4
Georgetown	20	181.4	9	219.6

development in Malaysia has always been recognised as one of the objectives of the various National Plans, but clearly there is still a long way to go before this objective can be achieved.

Notes

1. L.W. Jones, *North Borneo: Report on the Census of Population Taken on 10 August 1960* (Kuching: Government Printer, 1962).
2. L.W. Jones, *Sarawak: Census of Population Taken on 15 June 1960* (Kuching: Government Printer, 1962).
3. H. Fell, *1957 Population Census of the Federation of Malaya*, Report No. 14 Final Report (Kuala Lumpur: Department of Statistics, 1959).
4. R. Chander, *1970 General Report: Population Census of Malaysia*, Volume 1 (Kuala Lumpur: Department of Statistics, 1977).

5. Khoo Teik Huat, *1980 General Report of the Population Census*, Volume 1 (Kuala Lumpur: Department of Statistics, 1983).
6. Khoo Soo Gim, *1991 General Report of the Population Census*, Volume 1 (Kuala Lumpur: Department of Statistics, 1995).
7. Shaari bin Abdul Rahman, *2000 Population and Housing Census*, Population Distribution and Basic Demographic Characteristics (Kuala Lumpur: Department of Statistics, 2001).
8. Saw Swee-Hock, *The Population of Peninsular Malaysia* (Singapore: Singapore University Press, 1988).
9. "Malaysia to Restrict Foreign Labour", *Today*, 7 May 2004.
10. "160,000 Illegals Likely to Return to Indonesia", *Straits Times*, 25 October 2004.
11. Stephanie Phang, "Malaysia Faces a Labour Shortage", *International Herald Tribune*, 7 July 2005.
12. Lee Yong Leng, *Population and Settlement in Sarawak* (Singapore: Donald Moore, 1970).
13. Shaari bin Abdul Rahman, op. cit.
14. Saw Swee-Hock, "Urbanization in West Malaysia, 1911–70" in *Towards a Modern Asia: Aim, Resources and Strategies*, edited by Lim Teck Ghee and Vincent Lowe (Kuala Lumpur: Heinemann Educational Books, 1976).
15. Khoo Soo Gim, op. cit.
16. E.H.G. Dobby, "Settlement Patterns in Malaya", *Geographical Review* 32, no. 2 (April 1942).
17. Lim Heng Kow, *The Evolution of the Urban System in Malaya* (Kuala Lumpur: Universiti Malaya Press, 1978).
18. Haji Aziz bin Othman, *2,000 General Report of the Population and Housing Census* (Kuala Lumpur: Department of Statistics, 2005).

3

External Migration

The great ethnic diversity of the Malaysian population began to take shape after the penetration of European rule into the country. Malaysia has been one of the most important areas of migration ever since the establishment of British colonial rule in Penang in 1786 and in other parts of the country in the nineteenth century. The large and sustained immigration was mainly due to the demand for labour in the public works and primary production sectors, the excellent prospects for trade and commerce, and the law and order attendant on British rule. Such forces of attraction coupled with liberal immigration policies, were reinforced by equally strong repelling forces in the immigrants' countries of origin. Natural calamities, political upheavals, population pressure, and lack of economic opportunities induced the immigrants to leave their countries for Malaysia at a time when the supply of labour from the indigenous Malays was neither adequate nor forthcoming.

In the early days the immigrants would usually leave their families behind in their own countries and came to Malaysia not as permanent settlers but as "bird-of-passage". With their earnings, quite a number were able to send regular remittances to their families, made occasional visits home, and eventually returned to their countries after acquiring some wealth or on retirement. In the course of time, however, an increasing proportion of immigrants brought their families along, sent for their families or married local residents and remained in the country permanently. But their numbers did not alter the generally transient character of the population, which persisted until the outbreak of war in Malaysia in December 1941. The Japanese Occupation, the increasing supply of local labour in the postwar period, and the strict immigration control from the 1950s have put an end to large-scale immigration. At the same time an increasingly significant proportion of the prewar immigrants have come to regard Malaysia as their permanent home.

During the prewar period there were essentially three main streams of migration into Malaysia: the northern stream from China, the western stream from India, and the relatively less important stream from the then Dutch East Indies in the south. In view of the pronounced differences in magnitude, composition, mode of entry, and government regulations, it is perhaps more convenient to consider each stream separately. It should be mentioned that in official matters concerning migration, Malaysia and Singapore have until very recently been treated as a single unit governed by common law and regulations. In fact, up to the 1960s persons disembarking at one territory could proceed without hindrance to the next through the rail-and-road causeway, where movement between the two was completely free and unrestricted. It is therefore inevitable that the official statistics compiled during this period and presented in the various tables that follow refer to this combined area.

Another feature of migration in Malaysia is that until the outbreak of World War II the emigration of permanent residents to foreign countries has always been extremely insignificant. What this means is that the emigration figures presented in the various tables refer to persons who had in the first place migrated into Malaysia and were making short visits home or returning permanently to their motherland. In recent years migration appears to have assumed a new character, with some emigration from the minority races to foreign countries and secondly perceptibly more immigration from Indonesia than before.

CHINESE MIGRATION

While Chinese contacts with Malaysia date back to ancient times, it was after the establishment of British rule in the country in the early nineteenth century that marked the beginning of a long period of continuous Chinese migration. Despite the opposition of the Chinese Government to the immigration of its nationals to overseas territories, thousands of Chinese managed to come into the country during the first half of the nineteenth century.[1] By far the largest group were those who came to work as labourers in the pepper and tapioca farms and the gambier and sugar-cane plantations.

By the mid-nineteenth century, the immigration of Chinese had evolved into a well-organised system.[2] Potential immigrants were recruited in South China, particularly Kwangtung and Fukien provinces, by a returned immigrant known as *kheh thau* (headman), or by a professional recruiter. The *kheh thau* usually carried out the recruiting in his own village among persons known to him, and accompanied his *sin kheh* (new recruits) to Malaysia where he handed them over to a particular employer for whom he acted as an agent. As for the professional recruiter, he accompanied or sent his recruits to lodging-houses at the Chinese ports from which they were shipped to Malaysia. On arrival, the recruits were met by an agent of the lodging-houses in Malaysia, and eventually handed over to employers or labour contractors. The lodging-house owners acted a brokers, raking considerable profit from the recruitment and distribution of the immigrant labourers.

Whichever of the two methods the immigrants came by, they had their passage and other expenses paid for them by their employers who later recovered the amount from them, and they were therefore in debt on arrival. The system of Chinese immigration at that time was known to suffer from many evil practices, such as ill-treatment and exploitation. The first attempt at protecting and regulating Chinese immigration was made on 23 March 1877 when the colonial government enacted the Chinese Immigration Ordinance 1877. Under this Ordinance, a Chinese Protectorate Office was established in 1877. Conditions on board ships were improved, depots for receiving immigrants were set up, and recruits were licensed.[3]

A more important outcome was the emergence of Chinese indentured immigrants who signed formal contracts according to the provisions of the Ordinance in return for protection from the law. However, a large number of immigrants still preferred not to sign contracts, remaining legally free but still in the clutches of their employers as long as their debts remained.[4] In the 1880s, the proportion of indentured immigrants to total Chinese immigrants was slightly above 20 per cent, but by the 1910s it had fallen below 10 per cent. The original aim of introducing formal contracts to protect the immigrants was not achieved, and public opinion against the indentured system was also becoming more vocal in China. This led to the colonial government enacting the Labour Contracts Ordinance 1914 by which Chinese indentured immigration was abolished from 30 June 1914.[5]

The banning of indentured Chinese labour left the government with almost no legislation to deal with Chinese immigration, and for more than a decade the Chinese were free to enter the country. It was

in 1928 that the Immigration Restriction Ordinance 1928 was introduced
by the government to control immigration whenever the influx of
immigrants threatened to bring about unemployment or economic
distress.[6] This ordinance was first used in the World Depression when
a monthly quota on adult Chinese male immigrants was imposed on
1 August 1930. From an initial figure of 6,016 per month, the quota was
gradually reduced to 1,000 during the last five months of 1932. No
quota was placed on the immigration of Chinese women and children
under twelve years old.[7]

The Ordinance did not prove to be entirely satisfactory because it
could only be resorted to in emergencies and did not provide any control
over immigrants once they had landed. It was therefore replaced by the
Aliens Ordinance 1933 which came into force on 1 January 1933 and
transferred all functions concerning Chinese immigration from the
Chinese Protectorate Office to the new Immigration Department.[8] The
new legislation allowed the government to regulate the entry of aliens
and to register and control alien residents in the country. From 1 April
1933, the quota system of restricting adult Chinese male immigrants was
continued under the Aliens Ordinance until the outbreak of World War
II in December 1941. The immigration of Chinese women and children
continued to be exempted from any restriction up to 1 May 1938 when
a quota on Chinese women was imposed to ease the unemployed situation
at that time.[9] Immigration of Chinese was of course at a complete
standstill during the Japanese Occupation from December 1941 to
September 1945.

INDIAN MIGRATION

Contacts between the Indian sub-continent and the Malay Archipelago
go far back into ancient times when traders from both regions visited
one another's seaports. From the early seventh century such trading
relations were reinforced by cultural and religious influences from India
through the Hindu Empire of Srivijaya in Sumatra, which lasted from
AD 600 to AD 1000.[10] The movement of traders, missionaries and
settlers between the two regions continued into the periods of European
domination of the Straits of Malacca, but on a somewhat spasmodic and
meagre scale. Following the establishment of British rule in Malaysia in
the nineteenth century, the immigration of Indians became officially
countenanced and organised. Over the years, Indian immigration gradually

evolved into several distinct forms according to the needs and conditions prevailing in the country.

One of the earliest forms of Indian immigration was the inflow of convicts, introduced soon after the founding of the Straits Settlements of Singapore, Malacca and Penang by the East India Company with its governing body located in Bengal. The convicts constituted a cheap and ready supply of labour to the government in the construction of essential public works, such as roads, railways, bridges, canals, wharves and government buildings. After completing their sentences, they were repatriated to India, but a few were allowed to remain behind to seek new jobs and a fresh start in life. But convict immigration received much publicity and criticism while it lasted; it was finally prohibited after 1860 and those already here were repatriated to India by 1873.[11]

Indian indentured immigration appeared to have existed in the early nineteenth century, but it was not until 1872 that it was legalised and controlled by laws introduced by the Indian Government.[12] From 1884, it was brought under the control and protection of regulations in Malaysia. Immigrants imported under indenture were mainly employed in the cultivation of tapioca, tea, coffee and sugar-cane and in government departments dealing with the railway and public works. Notwithstanding the protection accorded by the law, a decreasing proportion of Indians came under this system owing to the lack of freedom in selecting and changing jobs. The diminishing usefulness of the system, the preference of the immigrants to the other systems, and the renewed public agitation against the system led to the government eventually banning Indian indentured immigration in December 1910.[13]

Another form of Indian immigration was known as the *kangany* system whereby the employers would send their own agent or *kangany* to India to recruit labourers. The *kangany*, usually a labourer already employed in the plantation, undertook to recruit workers from his village in India in return for a certain fee from his employer. But he advanced money to defray the expenses incurred by the recruits, who were willing to come but too poor to finance their own passage, and recovered the amount from their monthly wages. In most cases, the first month's wage was not sufficient to settle the debt completely so that the immigrants became the *kangany's* debtors from the outset, and hence subject to possible exploitation. Such immigrants, unlike the indentured ones, were legally not bound to serve their employer for a definite period, though they had to sign a promissory note for the advances made to them. The system was almost free from any restrictions until 1884 when *kangany* recruiters were required to be licensed.[14] In 1908 the system ceased to exist, having been modified and transformed under the assisted immigration system.

To increase the supply of labour in the early twentieth century, the government passed the Tamil Immigration Fund Ordinance 1907 by which the Indian Immigration Committee was constituted to manage the Indian Immigration Fund.[15] The fund, to which employers had to contribute, was used to finance the importation of Indian labourers. The Committee was responsible for regulating the flow of assisted immigrants by varying the number of recruiting licences and the recruiting allowance, or subsidy. Under the supervision of the Committee, Indian immigration evolved into two distinct types — recruited and non-recruited. Regardless of whether the immigrants came on their own or through licence — *kangany* recruiters, their expenses for the journey from India were met by the fund. These assisted immigrants were free from any debt and could change their job subject to one month's notice.

Apart from the above types of Indian immigration, there were the independent immigrants who were not subject to any government control. Such immigrants usually came on their own initiative and through their own financial means and arrangements. The years following the World Depression witnessed an increasing proportion of Indians coming in as independent immigrants, mainly to avoid the one week's detention at the quarantine camp.[16] This form of immigration was sharply curtailed from 15 June 1938 when the Indian Government's ban on the emigration of unskilled labourers to Malaysia was imposed.[17] It may be recalled that this time too, the other forms of Indian immigration had ceased to exist so that the only group of Indians to continue coming into the country after this date were independent immigrants other than the labouring class. The movement of Indian migration was completely halted by the outbreak of war on 8 December 1941, and remained at a standstill until the end of the Japanese Occupation in September 1945.

MALAY MIGRATION

Contacts between Malaysia and the numerous islands in the Indonesian archipelago date back to ancient times. The earliest recorded contacts were with the Srivijaya Empire (AD 600–1000), the capital of which was situated at Palembang in south Sumatra. Since then, there has been a continuous stream of settlers, labourers, traders and others from various parts of the archipelago into Singapore. While the main features of Chinese and Indian immigration during the nineteenth and twentieth centuries stand out quite clearly, Malay immigration in the same period is less easy to study, owing to the paucity of official British colonial documentation. More information was in fact available from Dutch sources pertaining to the Netherland Indies government.[18]

The movement of indentured immigrants from Indonesia into the country was governed by regulations introduced by the Government of the Netherland Indies. In 1887, the Netherland Indies Government prohibited the emigration of skilled and unskilled labour outside the country, but in special cases the Governor General could lift the ban if the recruitment took place in Java and Madura.[19] Permission was therefore given to some emigrants from these regions to proceed to Malaysia. The first official attempt at regulating and protecting indentured labour was made in 1909 when the Netherlands Indies Labour Enactment was put into force. This legislation was used to regulate the movement of indentured labour into Malaysia and to protect the workers by stipulating certain working and living conditions.

Indonesian indentured immigration outlived Chinese or Indian indentured immigration by many years partly because of the preference of the Dutch authorities for this system and partly because the relatively small numbers involved meant that abuses received little or no publicity. At the request of the Dutch authorities in 1927, and after protracted negotiations, Indonesian indentured immigration was finally abolished in 1932 when the Netherland Indies Labour Protection Enactment was abrogated. Another difference is that there was no government machinery instituted in Malaysia to organise and promote immigration from the Indonesian archipelago. Nevertheless, there was movement of people from the various parts of Indonesia into Malaysia over the years to work and trade. On account of their racial, religious and cultural similarities, the Indonesian immigrants mixed and intermarried freely with the local Malays. This process of assimilation has been ongoing so that the distinction between the two groups is now almost non-existent, and hence both are collectively known as Malays.

GROWTH OF FOREIGN-BORN POPULATION

We have observed the dominance of migration in the demographic history of Malaysia from the early nineteenth century to the outbreak of World War II in December 1941. This was followed by a lull of about five decades up to the 1990s, and thereafter a resurgence of large-scale migration surfaced and continued until nowadays. In contrast to the first wave of migration in the early years being monopolised by people from China and South Asia, the second wave was characterised by inward movement from nearby Indonesia and other Southeast Asian countries. In both periods, Malaysia was forced by the inadequate supply of labour from the local population to admit hoards of foreign workers into the country to work in the various sectors of the economy experiencing labour shortages.[20] On their part, the foreigners were driven by a desire to secure a regular and larger source of income to support their families back home.

In the course of time, many Chinese and South Indian workers in the first wave chose to stay in the country, thus contributing to the diminution of the Bumiputera population and the emergence of a multiracial community. In more recent years, the principal source of migrant workers emanates from nearby Indonesia where the people belong in the main to the same religious and ethnic background as the Malays. This has resulted in a gradual rise in the proportion of the Bumiputera population at the expense of the Chinese and the Indians, who were already experiencing a much lower level of fertility. No less important in the impact of current immigration concerns the prevalence of illegals, particularly the Indonesians, with all the attendant economic and social problems.

Unlike the availability of annual migration statistics in the early days before World War II, similar data for recent migration do not exist in official publications. The statistics that can be derived from completed forms submitted by persons arriving and departing the country are not very useful as they do not differentiate the genuine migrants from the tourists, visitors on business, and daily commuters across the Causeway. What we have are statistics on the birthplace of persons staying in Malaysia on census dates to provide us with an idea of the flow of the external in-migration to Malaysia. But information on external out-migration has never been collected in the censuses, and hence net international migration cannot be determined. There are some problems associated with the interpretation of the census in-migration data, and they will be dealt with in the respective sections that follow.

The large inflow of immigrants into the country at various times has resulted in a sizeable number of persons born outside Malaysia. Information on the country of birth, and hence the foreign-born population, has always been collected in the population censuses. The figures for the foreign-born population show the stock position of immigrants at the various census dates as against the dynamic situation depicted by annual figures. The census data are therefore defective to the extent that they do not take into account immigrants who have died during the intercensal period as well as those moving in and out of the country during the intervening period. Another limitation is that information on foreign-born persons is only available at rather long intervals of time as determined by the census dates.

The number of foreign-born persons enumerated at the four censuses conducted from 1970 to 2000 is laid out in Table 3.1. To put the issue of the foreign-born population in its proper perspective, we should bear in mind that the proportion of this group of persons has always remained at a small level during the whole period under consideration. The proportion stood at only 7.3 per cent in 1970, dropped to the low of 5.1 per cent in 1980, recovered slightly to 5.6 per cent in 1991, and continued upwards to 7.0 per cent in 2000. Moreover, some foreign-born persons have chosen to settle in the country, and elected to become Malaysian citizens.

TABLE 3.1
Distribution of Population by Local-Born and Foreign-Born, 1970–2000

Year	Population	Intercensal Income		Percentage of Total Population
		Number	Percentage	
Local-Born				
1970	9,675.0	—		92.7
1980	12,462.7	2,787.7	28.8	94.9
1991	16,574.6	4,111.9	33.3	94.4
2000	20,635.0	4,060.4	24.5	93.0
Foreign-Born				
1970	764.4	—	—	7.3
1980	673.4	−91.0	−11.9	5.1
1991	988.8	315.4	46.8	5.6
2000	1,563.3	574.5	58.1	7.0

In absolute terms, the number of foreign-born persons was reduced from 764,000 in 1970 to 673,400 in 1980, a drop of 91,000 on 11.9 per cent. This was caused partly by mortality particularly among the older foreign-born persons and partly by the outward movement of some foreign-born persons after the race riots of May 1969. Therefore, the number registered a notable rise of 315,400 or 46.8 per cent, bringing the figure to 988,800 in 1991. The increase continued at an accelerated pace during the latest intercensal period 1991–2000, recording a gain of 574,500 or 58.1 per cent to push the total foreign-born persons to the high of 1,563,300 in 2000. The foreign-born population enumerated in the 2000 census was fairly well represented by males and females, 54.3 per cent and 45.7 per cent respectively, unlike the very uneven sex ratio before World War II. The huge influx of foreign-born persons in recent years was triggered by the shortage of local workers in the plantation, construction and service sectors of the economy.

We will proceed to examine the distribution of foreign-born persons according to their country of birth as presented in Table 3.2. The figures show the marked variation in the growth rate recorded by the foreign-born persons from different countries and the resulting shift in their relative importance consequent on a change in the sources of recruiting foreign workers. The situation existing in the first pan-Malaysia Census held in 1970 reflects the character of the first wave of external in-migration during the pre-World War II years when the foreign workers came primarily from China and South Asia. In 1970 those born in China accounted for 54.5 per cent and those born in South Asia (India, Pakistan, Bangladesh and Sri Lanka) comprised 21.9 per cent.

With rigid immigration control and no demand for migrant workers during the early postwar years, the foreign-born persons from these two regions sustained a continuous reduction as attrition due to death affect the early, and by now elderly, foreigners. Those born in China were drastically reduced from 416,500 in 1970 to 283,600 in 1980, 153,000 in 1991, and finally to the low of 55,500 in 2000. Their relative importance was lowered from 54.5 per cent in 1970 to 42.1 per cent in 1980, 15.5 per cent in 1991 and 3.6 per cent in 2000. Those born in South Asia also experienced a decline, but at a slower pace, being lowered from 167,600 in 1970 to 112,900 in 1980, and 80,300 in 1991. This downward trend was reversed in 2000 when those originating from South Asia went up to 125,000, with those born in Bangladesh alone amounted to 92,200 or 73.8 per cent.

TABLE 3.2
Distribution of Foreign-Born Population by Country of Birth, 1970–2000

Country	1970	1980	1991	2000	Intercensal Change					
					Number			Percentage		
					1970–80	1980–91	1991–00	1970–80	1980–91	1991–00
Indonesia	76.5	124.5	423.1	660.4	48.0	298.6	237.3	62.7	239.8	56.1
Philippines	11.5	47.9	175.4	131.6	36.4	127.5	-43.8	316.5	266.2	25.0
Thailand	7.1	17.7	52.1	40.3	10.6	34.4	-11.8	149.3	194.4	-22.6
Singapore	50.2	51.8	52.4	42.1	1.6	0.6	-10.3	3.2	1.2	-19.7
China	416.5	283.6	153.0	55.5	-132.9	-130.6	-97.5	-31.9	-46.1	-63.7
South Asia	167.6	112.9	80.3	125.0	-54.7	-32.6	44.7	-32.6	-28.9	55.7
Others	34.9	29.8	52.6	59.3	-5.1	22.8	6.7	-14.6	76.5	12.7

The sustained economic growth from the late 1980s started the new wave of external in-migration from the Southeast Asian countries. The most remarkable growth was registered by those from Indonesia with similar religious and ethnic background as that of the Bumiputeras. From a modest number of 76,500 in 1970, the Indonesian-born persons ballooned to 124,500 in 1980, 423,100 in 1991, and 660,400 in 2000. Their relative importance jumped from 10.0 per cent to 42.2 per cent just within a span of thirty years. Philippines was another Southeast Asian country that benefited from the changes in the source of recruiting foreign workers. The number of foreign-born persons from this country rose sharply from 11,500 in 1970 to 47,900 in 1980 and 175,400 in 1991, after which it went up slightly to 131,600 in 2000. Their relative importance was raised from a mere 1.5 per cent to 8.4 per cent during the thirty-year period. An expansion of Thai-born persons was also noticeable, moving up from 7,100 in 1970 to 52,100 in 1991 and then down to 40,300 in 2000. Their relative importance was enhanced from 0.9 per cent to 2.6 per cent during the three decades. A very recent development occurred among the South Asian group where those from Bangladesh shot to prominence in 2000 with 92,200, accounting for 73.8 per cent of the South Asians and 5.9 per cent of the total foreign-born population.

ARRIVAL TIME OF FOREIGN-BORN POPULATION

The data we have been examining do not provide any idea as to when the persons from outside Malaysia enter the country. This type of information can be obtained by including an item on the year of first arrival in the census for all foreign-born respondents to complete, as has been done in some population censuses. This item was not included in the Malaysian censuses. Instead, an item on the place of usual residence five years prior to the census date was included in the 2000 Census. This item allows the compilation of statistics on foreign-born persons entering Malaysia, as external in-migrants, during the five-year period from 4 July 1995 to the census date of 5 July 2000.

Out of the total number of 1,563,310 foreign-born persons enumerated in the 2000 Census, some 327,971 or 21.2 per cent reported that their place of usual residence was outside Malaysia during the period up to five years prior to 5 July 2000. By way of subtraction from the total foreign-born persons, the other 1,231,339 or 78.8 per cent had their place of usual residence in foreign countries prior to 4 July 1995. This second group would consist of even those who entered the country before World War II. These figures derived from the place of usual residence do not include those who have died before the census date.

The same item used in the census can also be utilised to compile statistics on the country of usual residence (not birth) five years prior to the census day. These figures, presented in Table 3.3, refer only to those 327,971 foreign-born persons with their place of usual residence outside Malaysia during the five years prior to the census date. Those with their place of usual residence in Indonesia during the five-year period occupy a dominant position, numbering some 229,362 or 70.3 per cent. The other countries mentioned by the foreigners as their place of usual residence are somewhat insignificant. Bangladesh was mentioned by some 23,979 or 7.3 per cent, Philippines by 12,519 or 3.8 per cent, Singapore by 11,286 or 3.4 per cent, and Thailand by 9,207 or 2.8 per cent. Similar data by country for those with place of usual residence outside Malaysia prior to 4 July 1995 are not available. However, we know that those foreign-born persons residing outside Malaysia before World War II would originate from mainly China and South Asia.

TABLE 3.3

Distribution of Foreign-Born Population Entering Malaysia During July 1995–July 2000 by Country of Usual Residence and Sex

Country	Number			Percentage		
	Male	Female	Total	Male	Female	Total
Indonesia	125,873	103,489	229,362	65.4	76.3	69.9
Bangladesh	23,407	572	23,979	12.2	0.4	7.3
Philippines	5,991	6,528	12,519	3.1	4.8	3.8
Singapore	6,450	4,836	11,286	4.9	3.6	3.4
Thailand	4,645	4,562	9,207	2.4	3.4	2.8
South Asia	5,070	1,835	6,905	2.6	1.3	2.1
Japan	2,993	2,041	5,034	1.6	1.5	1.5
Brunei	1,790	1,530	3,320	0.9	1.1	1.0
Others	16,176	10,183	26,359	8.4	7.5	8.0
TOTAL	192,395	135,575	327,971	100.0	100.0	100.0

Some interesting contrasts are revealed by the separate figures for the two sexes and they are also given in Table 3.3. Among those with place of usual residence in Bangladesh during the same five-year period, there were 23,407 men as against only 577 women, a reflection of the country's tradition of not sending the women to work overseas. On the other hand, figures for the Philippines present quite a different picture with 5,991 men and 6,528 women, the only country sending more women than men to work in Malaysia. The Filipinos worked in the service industry as mainly domestic maids, while the men do not usually come to work in the plantation and construction sectors as in the case of the Bangladeshis and Indonesians. Among the Indonesians, there was a fair representation by the men and women, 125,893 and 107,489 respectively. The Indonesian men and women, being able to mingle easily with the local Bumiputera community, can be employed in a wide range of occupations.

The 327,971 foreign-born persons with place of usual residence outside Malaysia during the five years prior to 5 July 2000 were also classified according to the state where they were enumerated during the census day. The biggest group resided in Sabah with 75,701 or 22.8 per cent, followed by Selangor with 52,284 or 15.7 per cent and Johore with 51,831 or 15.6 per cent. The other east Malaysian state of Sarawak also had a sizeable number of 36,564 or 11.0 per cent. The fifth position was occupied by the Federal Territory of Kuala Lumpur where 22,631 or 6.8 per cent were staying. Relatively smaller groups were to be found in the other states.

REGIONAL DISTRIBUTION OF FOREIGN-BORN POPULATION

Persons born outside Malaysia have always congregated in those parts of the countries where jobs in certain sectors of the economy are readily available for foreign workers. This disposition comes out clearly in Table 3.4 showing the regional distribution of the 1,563,310 foreign-born persons enumerated in the 2000 Census. They have gravitated to work and stay in five main localities, Sabah, Selangor, Sarawak, Johore and Kuala Lumpur. The other nine states have been avoided by them. It should be noted that some foreigners are illegals, coming in and working without official documents.

By far the favourite state was the east Malaysian state of Sabah where some 414,421 or 26.4 per cent of the foreign-born persons were

TABLE 3.4
Distribution of Foreign-Born Population by
State and Country of Birth, 2000

State	No.	%	Percentage by Country					
			Indonesia	Philippines	Bangladesh	China	Others	
Johore	182,032	11.6	65.6	0.5	7.8	5.8	20.8	
Kedah	29,355	1.9	40.3	8.7	12.4	8.4	38.2	
Kelantan	22,801	1.5	15.3	0.1	0.9	2.1	81.2	
Malacca	28,061	1.8	55.4	0.6	11.1	11.7	21.2	
Negri Sembilan	38,172	2.4	54.8	0.5	11.1	11.7	21.9	
Pahang	54,553	3.5	70.7	0.3	5.0	7.3	16.7	
Penang	64,913	4.2	44.3	1.3	17.1	13.1	24.1	
Perak	54,714	3.5	45.1	0.7	11.6	15.6	26.7	
Perlis	3,612	0.2	12.6	0.3	1.1	6.5	79.6	
Sabah	414,421	26.4	65.5	32.2	0.0	0.6	1.6	
Sarawak	181,136	11.6	85.6	1.5	1.1	5.7	6.2	
Selangor	318,754	20.6	56.7	1.3	11.5	2.7	27.8	
Trengganu	18,971	1.2	50.7	0.5	3.9	2.7	42.1	
Kuala Lumpur	151,815	9.7	44.9	2.4	6.0	8.4	38.4	
Total	1,563,310	100.0	59.3	11.8	5.9	5.0	18.1	

residing in July 2000. Viewed from another perspective, these foreign-born persons constituted some 16.3 per cent of the total state population. Nearly all of them came from the two neighbouring countries, Indonesia in the south with 65.5 per cent and the Philippines in the north with 32.2 per cent. The latter percentage shows that Sabah was the only state with such a huge proportion of foreigners born in the Philippines. The neighbouring state of Sarawak has a fair number of foreign-born persons, 181,136 or 11.6 per cent. The more important feature refers to the overwhelming presence of those born in Indonesia, 85.6 per cent. Close proximity, due to long stretch of common borders, offers part of the explanation for the dominance of people from the Philippines and Indonesia in the two states.

The second most favoured state for foreign-born persons was Selangor which absorbed some 318,754 or 20.6 per cent. Many of them lived in this state, but travelled daily to work in the Federal Territory of Kuala Lumpur. The distribution of foreign-born persons according to their country of birth was not so imbalanced in the state. Slightly more than half, 56.7 per cent, were born in Indonesia, but those grouped under *Others* amounted to 27.8 per cent, which included India, Pakistan and Sri Lanka. Those born in Bangladesh, working mainly in the construction industry, constitute the third largest group, 11.5 per cent.

Though small in terms of land area, Kuala Lumpur was able to accommodate some 151,815 or 9.7 per cent foreign-born persons. And they emanated from a wider spread of birthplace, 44.9 per cent born in Indonesia, 8.4 per cent in China, 6.0 per cent in Bangladesh, and 2.4 per cent in the Philippines. The 38.4 per cent for *Others* would include those born in India, Pakistan and Sri Lanka. Most of the expatriates among the foreign-born persons engaged in business were located primarily in Kuala Lumpur. Those born in China and South Asia grouped under *Others* were probably the older immigrants who had taken up citizenship.

Johore with 11.6 per cent has taken in the same proportion of foreign-born persons as Sarawak. It has a large population, 65.6 per cent, of persons born in Indonesia; they were employed mainly in the rubber and palm oil plantations. A common characteristic displayed by the other nine states is the very low proportion of foreign-born persons, ranging from 0.2 per cent to not more than 3.5 per cent. The two northern states with a common land border with Thailand have an extremely high proportion for the *Others* group, 81.2 per cent in Kelantan and 79.6 per cent in Perlis. Undoubtedly, most of them were born in

Thailand, and among these Thailand-born were many Muslim Malays who would find it easier to live among the predominantly Malay population in the two states.

CITIZENSHIP OF FOREIGN-BORN POPULATION

The population born outside Malaysia comprised of two distinct groups, those who have become citizens and the others who have retained the citizenship of their own countries. Out of the total of 1,563,310 foreign-born population, some 557,715 or 35.7 per cent were Malaysian citizens and the other 1,005,590 or 64.3 per cent were non-citizens. It is obvious that the former group composed of immigrants who have entered and stayed in the country for a long time to be able to qualify for citizenship. The latter group, on the other hand, would consist of the more recent transient population who have come to the country with the sole aim of earning money rather than settling down permanently. They do not qualify to apply for Malaysian citizenship, or do not wish to apply even if they have the necessary qualifications.

In all the 2000 Census reports, the figures for the citizen population, whether local or foreign-born, have been presented according to ethnic groups but not the non-citizen population. Among the 557,715 foreign-born persons who had become citizens by the time of census day, some 228,288 or 40.9 per cent were Chinese and 63,556 or 11.4 per cent were Indians. These two groups of persons have resided in the country for quite some time and have even become citizens long ago. There were 214,413 or 40.2 per cent belonging to the Bumiputera group, and they were from Indonesia, Singapore, southern Thailand and southern Philippines.

Data for the two groups of foreign-born persons tabulated according to state are obtainable in the 2000 Census. The data given in Table 3.5 provide an insight into the differences in the regional distribution of citizens and non-citizens. Those who have become Malaysian citizens were concentrated in Selangor where some 147,700 or 26.5 per cent were residing, and also in Sarawak with 123,300 or 22.1 per cent. To a lesser extent, they were to be found in Kuala Lumpur with 14.6 per cent and Johore with 11.3 per cent.

A more notable feature refers to the much lesser spread of the 1,005,600 foreign-born non-citizens among the thirteen states. An extremely high proportion, 36.2 per cent, were residing in Sabah, and 17.0 per cent in Selangor and 11.9 per cent in Johore. These three states

TABLE 3.5
Distribution of Foreign-Born Population by State and Citizenship, 2000

State	Number ('000)		Percentage	
	Citizens	Non-Citizens	Citizens	Non-Citizens
Johore	62.8	119.3	11.3	11.9
Kedah	9.0	20.4	1.6	2.0
Kelantan	4.2	18.6	0.8	1.9
Malacca	10.9	17.2	1.9	1.7
Negri Sembilan	9.6	28.5	1.7	2.8
Pahang	11.6	42.9	2.1	4.3
Penang	20.4	44.5	3.7	4.4
Perak	19.6	35.1	3.5	3.5
Perlis	1.1	2.5	0.2	0.3
Sabah	49.9	364.5	9.0	36.2
Sarawak	123.3	54.9	22.1	5.5
Selangor	147.7	171.0	26.5	17.0
Trengganu	5.3	13.7	1.0	1.4
Kuala Lumpur	82.3	69.5	14.8	6.9
Total	557.7	1,005.6	100.0	100.0

accounted for two-thirds of these foreigners. Many of them were in fact illegal immigrants working in certain sectors of the economy suffering from acute shortage of labour.[21] As discussed earlier in Chapter 2 dealing with population growth and distribution, attempts have been made in recent years to repatriate the illegals back to their own countries.

Notes

1. Victor Purcell, *The Chinese in Southeast Asia* (London: Oxford University Press, 1951).
2. A more detailed account is given in W.L. Blythe, "Historical Sketch of Chinese Labour in Malaya", *Journal of the Malayan Branch of the Royal Asiatic Society* 20, Part 1 (June 1947).
3. R.N. Jackson, *Immigrant Labour and Development of Malaya* (Kuala Lumpur: Government Printer, 1961).
4. C.W.C. Parr, *Report of Protector of Chinese 1914* (Singapore: Government Press, 1915).

5. Straits Settlements, *Report of Protector of Chinese 1914* (Singapore: Government Press, 1915).

6. Norman Parmer, *Colonial Labour Policy and Administration* (New York: Association for Asian Studies, 1960).

7. Straits Settlements, *Report of Protector of Chinese, 1932* (Singapore: Government Press, 1934).

8. Straits Settlements, *Report of the Immigration Department, 1933* (Singapore: Government Press, 1935).

9. Straits Settlement and Federated Malay States, *Report of the Immigration Department 1938* (Singapore: Government Press, 1940).

10. D.G.E. Hall, *A History of Southeast Asia* (London: Macmillan, 1958).

11. Straits Settlements, *Annual Report on the Administration of the Straits Settlements, 1860–1861*.

12. J. Geoghegan, *Note on Emigration from India* (Calcutta: Government Press, 1873).

13. Straits Settlements and Federated Malay States, *Report on Indian Immigration, 1910* (Singapore: Government Press, 1912).

14. N.E. Marjoribanks and A.K.G. Ahmad Tambi Marakkaya, *Report on Indian Labour Emigration to Ceylon and Malaya* (Madras: Government Press, 1917).

15. Parmer, op. cit.

16. Malaya, *Report of the Labour Department, 1938* (Singapore: Government Press, 1940).

17. Ibid.

18. Tungku Shamsul Bahrin, "Indonesian Labour in Malaya", *Kajian Ekonomi Malaysia* 2, no. 1 (June 1965).

19. *Proceedings of the 24th Session of the National Labour Conference* (Geneva, 1937).

20. Saw Swee-Hock, "Trends and Differentials in International Migration in Malaya", *Ekonomi* 4, no. 1 (December 1963).

21. "KL Targets 1 Million Illegal Immigrants in Crackdown", *Straits Times*, 15 July 2006.

4

Internal Migration

The movement of people within Malaysia has assumed greater significance as a result of the official concern about the unbalanced distribution of the population among the various parts of the country. This concern was explicitly expressed in the development plans adopted from the early 1970s onwards, and specific strategies were spelled out to, among other things, redistribute the population. The plans seek to distribute the population to sparsely settled rural areas with agricultural potential, to spread out the urban population more evenly throughout the country, and to rearrange the population with the view of attaining greater economic balance among the major communities. The underlying purpose of the last strategy as stated in the Third Malaysia Plan was to free the Bumiputeras from their dependence on subsistence agriculture and to allow them to participate in the "modern rural and urban sectors of the economy at all levels".[1] In fact, the Second Malaysia Plan as spelled out the overall aim of the population policies was meant to achieve "economic balance between urban and rural areas and to eliminate the identification of race with vocation as well as location".[2]

Internal migration may be defined as a change of residence from one community or geographical unit to another within the national boundaries. The movement of people within the country can be examined in terms of the following categories:

1. Migration among the thirteen states, known as inter-state migration.
2. Migration among the various districts within a particular state. This is known as intra-state migration at the district level.
3. Migration among different urban and rural areas. This can be classified into urban-urban, urban-rural, rural-urban, and rural-rural.

An urban area is defined as a conurbation with 10,000 or more inhabitants.[3] The rural-urban type of movement is more commonly known as urbanisation. Each state is sub-divided into smaller units known as districts, with different number of districts in each of the thirteen states. In view of the national aim of achieving a more balanced socio-economic development among the various ethnic groups and among the various regions of the country, the population censuses have always collected statistics that can enable us to study internal migration.

LIFETIME INTER-STATE MIGRATION

One way of measuring the volume and direction of inter-state migration is the place-of-birth method based on census data on the state of birth of respondents at the census dates.[4] An explanation of a few key terms used in this method would be helpful. Lifetime in-migrants refer to persons enumerated in a given state at a particular census and born outside the state of enumeration but within the national boundaries. Lifetime out-migrants refer to persons born in a given state and enumerated outside the state but again within the national boundaries. Lifetime net migrants would refer to the difference between the number of lifetime in-migrants and the member of lifetime out-migrants at the census date. When we deal with inter-state migration that occurred during intercensal periods, the three terms so defined would be used.

In Table 4.1 are laid out the estimates of inter-state migration based on the place-of-birth method using the relevant data collected in the last three censuses. Before commenting on the figures, we should bear in mind the inherent shortcomings of the method. Firstly, it does not cover the inter-state movement of foreign-born persons, and hence does not reflect the total picture of inter-state movement that has occurred in the country.[5] However, this defect is not so serious since the local-born population covered by this method amounted to 94.9 per cent in 1980, 94.4 per cent in 1991, and 93.0 per cent in 2000. Secondly, the method takes into consideration only the final destination of the inter-state moves as observed during the census dates, and does not take into consideration those intermediate moves to other states as well as those moves out of a state and back to it again by the time of the next census date.

According to the figures in Table 4.1, the number of in-migrants in all the states in Malaysia rose from 1,865,400 in 1980 to 3,200,200 in

TABLE 4.1
Lifetime Inter-State Migration, 1980–2000

State	In-Migrants			Out-Migrants			Net Migrants		
	1980	1991	2000	1980	1991	2000	1980	1991	2000
Johore	133.5	245.0	340.7	159.3	303.1	377.8	-25.9	-58.0	-37.1
Kedah	90.8	151.5	219.3	198.0	329.2	388.8	-107.2	-177.7	-169.6
Kelantan	32.8	60.7	50.2	121.3	217.4	358.1	-88.4	-156.7	-307.8
Malacca	58.0	88.2	117.7	149.7	228.2	256.7	-91.7	-139.9	-120.4
Negri Sembilan	98.4	178.3	221.6	160.2	227.1	267.9	-61.8	-48.8	-46.3
Pahang	236.1	320.6	347.7	73.6	143.8	227.4	163.2	176.8	120.4
Penang	127.2	197.5	239.5	148.0	210.4	251.7	-20.8	-12.9	-12.3
Perak	136.1	204.2	212.0	388.8	631.5	793.4	-252.7	-427.3	-581.4
Perlis	23.4	40.8	41.4	26.8	43.5	58.9	-3.4	-2.6	-17.5
Sabah	26.7	77.1	83.5	9.9	45.1	103.4	16.8	32.0	-19.9
Sarawak	19.5	54.9	26.7	17.4	48.3	93.7	2.1	-13.4	-66.9
Selangor	409.5	998.6	1,788.0	229.5	250.6	255.0	180.1	748.0	1,533.1
Trengganu	52.3	89.5	103.5	59.8	99.5	152.8	-7.5	-10.0	-49.3
Kuala Lumpur	420.4	515.3	538.8	123.2	422.5	745.0	297.2	90.8	-206.2
Labuan	—	—	—	—	—	4.5	—	—	20.1
Malaysia	1,865.4	3,200.2	4,330.6	1,865.4	3,200.2	4,330.6	0	0	0

1991, up by 1.7 per cent. This increase was reduced to 1.4 per cent during the next period 1991–2000 when the number rose to 4,330,600 in 2000. The differences in the increase during the two intercensal periods naturally have an impact on the magnitude and pattern of lifetime in-migrants among the 13 states, plus Kuala Lumpur. During the intercensal period 1980–91, lifetime in-migrants increased by nearly thrice in Sabah and Sarawak, one-and-a-half times in Selangor, and almost twice in Kelantan, Malacca and Negri Sembilan. Following the slowdown in lifetime in-migrants for the whole of the country, the next intercensal period witnessed a more modest increase in the various states. The largest increase managed to reach only 1.8 per cent, and this was recorded by Selangor. There were even two states, Kelantan and Sarawak, which recorded a decrease in lifetime in-migrants.

It is obvious that the distribution of lifetime in-migrants according to the states would alter in these years. The two most popular places for in-migrants were Selangor and Kuala Lumpur. In 1980 Kuala Lumpur and Selangor occupied the first and second position, but the position was reversed in 1991 and 2000 as the limited area in Kuala Lumpur imposed a severe restriction on the expansion of its population, which naturally spillover in Selangor. The third position was retained by Pahang during these years. The least popular state for lifetime in-migrants shifted from Sarawak in 1980 to Perlis in 1991, and then back again to Sarawak in 2000. In the long haul, the distribution of in-migrants has became more lopsided, with Selangor becoming the dominant state for inter-state migrants.

The relatively small rise in lifetime out-migrants in Selangor, from 229,500 in 1980 to 255,000 in 2000, as compared to the spectacular increase from 123,200 to 745,000 during the same period in Kuala Lumpur confirms the huge inflow of in-migrants in Selangor being due to the movement of people from Kuala Lumpur into Selangor. During the period 1980–1991, the largest increase in out-migrants was experienced in Sabah (355.6 per cent), Sarawak (242.9 per cent), and Kuala Lumpur (177.6 per cent). A moderate increase was recorded in the other states. During the latest period, only Sabah managed to record an increase of slightly more than two-fold, with all the other states recording less than this rate. Througout the whole period, the top spot for out-migrants was Perak, but the second spot shifted from Selangor in 1980 to Kuala Lumpur in 1991 and 2000.

Of greater significance are the figures for lifetime net migrants, which reflect the relative attractiveness of the various regions for internal migrants and the different levels of socio-economic development among the various parts of the country. Furthermore, the data laid out in Table 4.1 are significant in the sense that they constitute another factor, in addition to fertility, mortality and internal migration, that had determined the rate of population growth in the various states during the intercensal periods. The pattern of life-time net migrants has not altered significantly during the years. In 1980 a substantial net gain was recorded in Kuala Lumpur (297,300), Selangor (180,100) and Pahang (163,200), with Sabah and Sarawak benefiting from a small net gain. By 1991 the number of states with net gain was reduced to only 4 when Sarawak registered a net loss. This was further reduced to only 2 in 2000 when Selangor registered the spectacular figure of 1,533,100, way ahead of the second position of 120,400 for Pahang.

The above discussion of the absolute numbers does not reflect the extent to which the state population was subjected to lifetime internal migration, which can only be measured by the rates given in Table 4.2. These rates, expressed in terms of the number of lifetime migrants as a percentage of state total population, attempt to measure the intensity of internal migration in each state by taking into account the size of the population which varies appreciably among the various states. In 1980 the rate of lifetime in-migration reached the highest level in Kuala Lumpur (46.1 per cent), followed by Pahang (31.0 per cent). The next census held in 1991 saw Kuala Lumpur retaining its top position, but the second position now belonged to Selangor. Another shift occurred in 2000 when Selangor moved to the top, pushing Kuala Lumpur to the second spot. The two eastern states of Sarawak and Sabah have always been subjected to the two lowest rate of in-migration.

In 1980 the rate of lifetime out-migration was the highest in Malacca (33.9 per cent), with Negri Sembilan (29.2 per cent) taking up the second position. Malacca continued to be the top state for out-migration in 1991, but this time the second spot was occupied by Kuala Lumpur. By 2000 Kuala Lumpur had moved up to the top spot. Sarawak and Sabah were again exposed to the lowest level of out-migration, a reflection of their geographical distance from the states in West Malaysia and the retention of in-migration controls by these two states.[6]

A fairly clear trend is displayed by the figures for the rate of lifetime net migration. In 1980 there were nine states registering a loss of lifetime net migrants, and this was raised to ten in 1991 and twelve in 2000. The state receiving the lifetime migrants from these states was Selangor

TABLE 4.2
Percentage of Inter-State Migration to State Population, 1980–2000

State	In-Migrants			Out-Migrants			Net Migrants		
	1980	1991	2000	1980	1991	2000	1980	1991	2000
Johore	8.5	11.9	13.2	10.2	14.7	14.6	-1.6	-2.8	-1.4
Kedah	8.4	11.6	14.0	18.2	15.3	24.7	-10.0	-13.7	-10.8
Kelantan	3.8	5.1	3.9	14.1	18.4	27.8	-10.3	-13.3	-23.9
Malacca	13.1	17.5	19.4	33.9	45.3	42.4	-20.8	-17.8	-23.0
Negri Sembilan	17.9	25.8	26.7	29.2	32.8	32.3	-11.3	-7.1	-5.6
Pahang	31.0	30.9	28.3	9.6	13.9	18.5	21.4	17.0	9.8
Penang	14.2	18.7	19.4	16.5	19.9	20.4	-2.3	-1.2	-1.0
Perak	7.9	10.9	10.7	22.5	33.8	40.2	-14.6	-22.9	-29.5
Perlis	16.1	22.2	20.9	18.5	23.7	29.7	-2.6	-1.4	-8.8
Sabah	2.8	3.3	2.4	1.0	2.3	4.0	1.8	1.0	-1.6
Sarawak	1.6	2.1	1.3	1.4	3.0	4.7	0.2	-0.8	-3.3
Selangor	28.8	43.5	45.2	16.1	10.9	6.5	12.6	32.6	38.8
Trengganu	10.0	11.7	11.8	11.4	13.0	17.4	-1.4	-1.3	-5.6
Kuala Lumpur	46.1	45.4	41.8	13.5	37.4	57.1	32.6	8.0	-15.8
Malaysia	14.3	18.3	19.5	14.3	18.3	19.5	0	0	0

which saw its rate of net gain in in-migration going up from 12.6 per cent to 38.8 per cent during the last twenty years. The other state that also attracted migrants was Pahang, but in this case the rate fell steadily from 21.4 per cent to 9.8 per cent during the same period. More remarkable is the trend displayed by Kuala Lumpur. Starting with the highest gain of net migration equivalent to 32.6 per cent, the rate was quickly lowered to 8.0 per cent in 1991 and was even reversed to a negative rate of 15.8 per cent in 2000.

FIVE-YEAR INTER-STATE MIGRATION

Information on more recent internal migration was collected in the 2000 Census through a question on the usual place of residence five years prior to the date of enumeration.[7] The inter-state migrants computed from these statistics refer to those respondents whose current place of residence at the time of the census was in a different state from that of their usual place of residence five years ago. The figures are for the five-year period from 4 July 1995 to 5 July 2000, and are therefore known as five-year inter-state migration. Unlike lifetime internal migration, which does not include those born outside Malaysia, the figures for five-year internal migration cover those born inside as well as outside the country. However, to be considered as an internal migrant the foreign-born persons must have entered the country at least five years prior to the census date, and would therefore have a usual place of usual residence in Malaysia instead of outside Malaysia as in the case of external migrants.

Three types of internal migration flows can be identified. Inter-state in-migrants refers to persons who have moved from another state to reside in the state where they were enumerated. Inter-state out-migrants refer to persons who have moved out of the state of enumeration to reside in another state. Inter-state net migrants refer to the difference between the number of in-migrants and out-migrants. If the number of in-migrants exceeds out-migrants in a state, the result would be a net gain in inter-state migration or net in-migration. In the reverse case, the result would be a net loss in inter-state migration or net out-migration.

The data for the inter-state migration of the population during the five-year period 1995–2000 are presented in Table 4.3. The number of inter-state migrants in Malaysia during this period totalled about 1.06 million as against the 1.15 million during the 1986–1991 period. A better

TABLE 4.3
Five-Year Inter-State Migration, 1995–2000

State	Number ('000)			Rate		
	In-Migrants	Out-Migrants	Net Migrants	In-Migrants	Out-Migrants	Net Migrants
Johore	107.4	88.2	19.2	4.2	3.4	0.7
Kedah	65.7	78.0	-12.3	4.2	5.0	-0.8
Kelantan	29.2	88.0	-58.8	2.3	6.8	-4.6
Malacca	40.7	37.8	2.9	6.7	6.2	0.5
Negri Sembilan	69.1	51.3	-17.8	8.3	6.2	2.1
Pahang	61.7	76.0	-14.4	5.0	6.2	-1.2
Penang	65.5	51.9	13.6	5.3	4.2	1.1
Perak	70.3	121.3	-50.9	3.6	6.1	-2.6
Perlis	10.7	13.6	-2.9	5.4	6.9	-1.5
Sabah	32.2	53.0	-20.8	1.0	1.9	-0.9
Sarawak	19.3	43.2	-24.0	1.0	2.2	-1.2
Selangor	344.4	107.5	236.9	8.7	2.7	6.0
Trengganu	34.5	46.6	-12.1	3.9	5.3	-1.4
Kuala Lumpur	106.3	200.5	-94.2	8.1	15.4	-7.2
Total	1,057.0	1,057.0	0.0	4.8	4.8	0.0

indicator of the magnitude of this internal movement is of course the rate of inter-state migration defined as the percentage of inter-state migrants to the total population in the state. The proportion of persons reporting a different state of residence five years ago in 1995 as compared to their state of residence in 2000 was 4.8 per cent. This rate was lower than the 6.6 per cent experienced during the 1986–1991 period.

Selangor, with 344,400 in-migrants, stands out as the most popular state for internal migrants from other states. Way behind was Johore with 107,400 and Kuala Lumpur with 106,300. Out-migrants reached the highest level in Kuala Lumpur with 200,500, followed by Perak with 121,300 and Selangor with 107,500. Inter-state migration during the five-year period 1995–2000 was dominated by Selangor, the recipient of a huge inflow of migrants amounting to some 236,900. The other three states receiving a net gain of inter-state migrants were rather unimportant, Johore with 19,200, Penang with 13,600, and Malacca with 2,900. The greatest loss in net migrants took place in Kuala Lumpur, losing 94,200.

The figures for the inter-state migration rate, also given in Table 4.3, indicate that the three highest rate of in-migration was experienced by Selangor (8.7 per cent), Negri Sembilan (8.3 per cent), and Kuala Lumpur (8.1 per cent). The lowest rate of in-migration was recorded in the two eastern states of Sabah and Sarawak, both with 1.0 per cent. A completely different pattern was displayed by the figures for the out-migration rate. By far the highest rate of out-migration occurred in Kuala Lumpur, as high as 15.4 per cent. This is in sharp contrast to the second highest of 6.9 per cent registered by Perlis. The outcome of these diverging patterns meant that five states attained a positive rate of net inter-state migration during the five-year period. They were Selangor (6.0 per cent), Negri Sembilan (2.1 per cent), Penang (1.1 per cent), Johore (0.7 per cent), and Malacca (0.5 per cent).

MIGRATION ORIGIN AND DESTINATION

Having seen the evolution of the pattern of five-year inter-state migration into one whereby movement has been essentially outwards from eight states and Kuala Lumpur to the other states, we will proceed a step further by looking at the direction of migration streams. In Table 4.4 we have provided the data for the state of origin of in-migrants to Selangor, Johore and Negri Sembilan. With regard to the most popular state of Selangor, the principal source of migration was from the neighbouring Federal Territory of Kuala Lumpur, which contributed an incredibly huge number of 131,400 or 38.2 per cent. This is a clear confirmation of our earlier statement that there has been a conspicuous outflow of residents from the crowded and expansive houses in Kuala Lumpur into mainly new housing developments in nearby Selangor. The other states contributing a fair number of migrants were Perak (41,300), Johore (27,400), Kelantan (25,800), and Pahang (23,500).

The people who moved into Selangor went not only for more space but for jobs in the manufacturing sector. Johore, the second most popular state for migrants, was the recipient of 15,000 migrants from Perak, 12,100 from Kelantan, 11,400 from Selangor, and 11,300 from Kuala Lumpur. As for Negri Sembilan the in-migrants came mainly from the neighbouring state of Selangor (16,000), Kuala Lumpur (10,500), and Johore (9,200).

We will now look at the other side of inter-state migration stream in Table 4.5 giving the data for the destination of out-migrants from three

TABLE 4.4
Five-Year Inter-State In-Migrants to Major Net Gaining States by State of Origin, 1995–2000

State of Origin	State of Destination					
	Selangor		Johore		Negri Sembilan	
	Number ('000)	Percentage	Number ('000)	Percentage	Number ('000)	Percentage
Johore	27.4	8.0	—	—	9.2	13.4
Kedah	16.4	4.7	6.5	6.1	3.0	4.4
Kelantan	25.8	7.5	12.1	11.3	4.6	6.6
Malacca	10.6	3.1	7.6	7.1	5.3	7.7
Negri Sembilan	17.9	5.2	8.2	7.6	—	—
Pahang	23.5	5.8	10.8	10.0	5.7	8.2
Penang	11.1	3.2	4.1	3.8	1.4	2.1
Perak	41.3	12.0	15.0	13.9	5.1	7.4
Perlis	2.4	0.7	0.9	0.8	0.5	0.7
Sabah	14.9	4.1	5.7	5.3	2.4	3.6
Sarawak	9.7	2.8	7.4	6.9	3.0	4.4
Selangor	—	—	11.4	10.6	16.0	23.2
Trengganu	12.0	3.5	6.6	6.2	2.5	3.6
Kuala Lumpur	131.4	38.2	11.3	10.5	10.5	14.9
Total	344.4	100.0	107.4	100.0	69.1	100.0

main states. The tremendous popularity of Selangor to the out-migrants from Perak exerted a pronounced impact on the direction of population outflow from this state, viz. Penang (15,900), Johore (915,000), and Kuala Lumpur (14,300).

A very lopsided pattern of the destination of out-migrants from Kuala Lumpur was indicated in the figures laid out in Table 4.5. It should not come as a surprise that the principal direction of the out-migrants was towards Selangor which received 131,400 migrants, constituting 65.5 per cent of the total out-migrants from Kuala Lumpur. The other less important destinations were to Johore (11,300), Perak (10,800) and Negri Sembilan (10,300). A more balanced pattern of the destination of out-migrants from the northern state of Kelantan is depicted by the data provided in the same table. Not greatly different number of out-migrants

TABLE 4.5

Five-Year Inter-State Out-Migrants from Major Net Losing States by State of Destination, 1995–2000

State of Origin	State of Origin					
	Perak		Kuala Lumpur		Kelantan	
	Number ('000)	Percentage	Number ('000)	Percentage	Number ('000)	Percentage
Johore	15.0	12.3	11.3	5.6	12.1	13.8
Kedah	10.2	8.4	6.5	3.2	4.5	5.1
Kelantan	2.8	2.3	3.4	1.7	—	—
Malacca	2.9	2.4	5.6	2.8	2.5	2.5
Negri Sembilan	5.1	4.2	10.3	5.1	4.6	5.2
Pahang	5.9	4.9	7.0	3.5	8.7	9.9
Penang	15.9	13.1	4.9	0.5	0.7	0.8
Perak	—	—	10.8	5.4	5.3	6.0
Perlis	1.4	1.2	0.9	0.5	0.7	0.8
Sabah	3.2	2.7	2.8	1.3	1.6	1.8
Sarawak	1.4	1.2	2.2	1.1	1.4	1.6
Selangor	41.3	34.0	131.4	65.5	25.4	29.4
Trengganu	1.9	1.6	3.4	1.7	7.9	8.9
Kuala Lumpur	14.3	11.8	—	—	8.0	9.1
Total	121.3	100.0	200.5	100.0	88.0	100.0

moved to Selangor (25,400), Johore (12,100), Pahang (8,700), Kuala Lumpur (8,000), and Trengganu (7,900).

Bearing in mind the geographical relationship of the above states that proved to be popular for out-migrants from a particular state, it would appear that distance is an important factor that determines the magnitude of inter-state migration. This is in accordance with one of the migration laws, which states that the rate of migration between two points will be increasingly related to the distance between these points.[8] Immediate neighbouring states were more attractive to internal migrants, as has been mentioned earlier.

The other factor that has exerted a huge influence is the irresistible pull of big cities with better job opportunities and superior living conditions. This has become increasingly more important as the impact of modernisation and globalisation reinforces the attractiveness of city

life. This is the key explanation for the popularity of the primate city of
Kuala Lumpur and Selangor for out-migrants from the other parts of the
country. It should be noted that there was the third pull-factor that
emerged in Malaysia and this refers to the rural development projects as
evidenced by the fair number of out-migrants from other states to
Pahang with the greatest number of such projects. Movement of
inhabitants among Kuala Lumpur and the eleven states in West Malaysia
is completely free, but movement into Sarawak and Sabah is regarded as
a local matter under the control of these two states.[9]

FIVE-YEAR INTER-DISTRICT MIGRATION

For administrative purposes, each of the thirteen states in Malaysia has
been divided into smaller areas known as districts under the charge of
a district officer. As to be expected, the number of districts in the state
would be determined by the land area, and to some extent the population
size. The Federal Territory of Kuala Lumpur constitutes one single
administrative unit, and there is therefore no such thing as inter-district
migration within this unit. Moreover, the smallest state of Perlis was
regarded in the population censuses as one district for the purpose of
collection of information at the district level.[10] Kuala Lumpur and Perlis
do not therefore feature at all in Table 4.6 showing the five-year inter-
district migration with each state. The figures provided in this table are
derived from the same data employed to obtain the five-year inter-state
migration discussed previously.

For Malaysia as a whole, the number of inter-district migrants
within the states rose from 590,000 during the few-year period 1975–
1980 to 928,000 during the following period 1986–1991, but fell back to
600,800 during the most recent period 1995–2000. The rate of inter-
district migration as measured by the proportion to the total population
advanced from 4.5 per cent to 5.3 per cent, and then dwindled to the low
of 2.7 per cent at the end of the whole thirty-year period.

The huge increase in the overall inter-district migration from the
first five-year period to the second five-year period naturally led to
almost all the twelve states benefiting from an increase in inter-district
migrants. Substantial increase was experienced by Sabah, Kedah,
Selangor and Sarawak. Negri Sembilan was the only state that recorded
a decrease, though a minor one from 29,200 to 28,600. The picture was
completely reversed during the third five-year period 1995–2000 when

TABLE 4.6

Five-Year Inter-District Migrants Within State by State, 1975–2000

State	Number ('000)			Rate			Number of Districts in 2000
	1975–1980	1986–1991	1995–2000	1975–1980	1986–1991	1995–2000	
Johore	94.2	108.4	61.4	6.0	5.3	2.4	8
Kedah	18.4	63.3	35.0	4.5	4.9	2.2	11
Kelantan	39.8	65.5	30.3	4.6	5.6	2.4	10
Malacca	9.2	11.3	9.3	2.1	2.2	1.6	3
Negri Sembilan	29.2	28.6	18.6	5.3	4.1	2.2	7
Pahang	45.8	54.3	31.6	6.0	5.2	2.6	11
Penang	36.3	40.0	37.1	2.9	3.8	3.0	5
Perak	70.4	75.3	34.6	4.1	4.0	1.8	9
Sabah	53.8	166.3	121.3	5.7	9.6	4.9	24
Sarawak	100.0	175.8	83.5	8.1	10.7	4.2	29
Selangor	50.2	103.9	113.6	3.5	4.5	2.9	9
Trengganu	22.7	35.3	24.1	4.4	4.6	2.7	7
Total	590.0	928.0	600.8	4.5	5.3	2.7	133

the overall inter-district migration dropped back to the level observed in the first period. The only state that went against the common down trend was Selangor which saw a slight rise in inter-district migrant from 103,900 in the second period to 113,600 in the third period.

During the first five-year period, the highest rate of inter-district migration was chalked up by Sarawak with 8.1 per cent, and Sabah was the third highest with 5.7 per cent. By the second five-year period, these two states emerged clearly as the two top states, 10.7 per cent for Sarawak and 9.6 per cent for Sabah. They continued to maintain their top two positions during the latest period, though a somewhat lower level. Given that these two eastern states contain more than twice the number of districts as compared to the other states in Malaysia, it is not surprising that they should always experience a higher intensity of inter-district migration. Another explanation can be traced to the residents finding it rather difficult to move across the South China Sea to West Malaysia. They would, instead, choose the easier path of moving to another district in their own state.

URBAN AND RURAL MIGRATION

The availability of relevant data in the recent census reports enables us to study the movements of the population between and within rural and urban areas, which occupy a central position in the study of internal migration in a country. The four specific types of movements that will be investigated are urban to urban, urban to rural, rural to urban, and rural to rural. The data on the usual place of residence five years prior to the census date were also tabulated according to rural and urban areas based on the cut-off point of 10 000 persons. The four types of five-year internal population flows for the two periods 1986–1991 and 1995–2000 are presented in Table 4.7. It should be mentioned that these four types of internal migration cover those movements within each state as well as those across state boundaries.

The figures show that some 1,024,500 persons have participated in internal movements between and within rural and urban areas during the period 1986–1991. The most striking feature refers to urban-urban migration constituting the major flow, 513,300 or 50.1 per cent of the total flow during this period. This should not come as a surprise considering the large pool of population in the urban area, 50.7 per cent in 1991. Besides, movements of inhabitants among the many small conurbations with a shade over 10,000 persons would be included in this type of internal migration.

The second type of movement viz. urban to rural, was participated by 212,100 migrants, accounting for 20.7 per cent of the total movements in 1986–1991. This was followed closely by rural to urban migration, 175,500 migrants or 17.1 per cent. The significant aspect of this relatively

TABLE 4.7

Five-Year Urban and Rural Migration, 1986–2000

Type of Flow	Number ('000)		Percentage	
	1936–1991	1995–2000	1986–1991	1995–2000
Urban to Urban	513.3	573.7	50.1	68.8
Urban to Rural	212.1	111.7	20.7	13.4
Rural to Urban	175.5	106.7	17.1	12.8
Rural to Rural	123.7	41.3	12.1	5.0
Total	1,024.5	833.4	100.0	100.0

small volume of movement implies that the recent growth in the population of urban centres was engendered more by natural increase and external in-migration from neighbouring countries. Rural to rural migration, 123,700 or 12.1 per cent, was the least important because it did not make much sense to move from one rural place to another, with no good prospect for better jobs and standard of living.

Comparative figures for the period 1995–2000 reveal some interesting changes in the four types of internal migration. In the first place, there was a reduction in the total volume of this migration, being lowered from 1,024,500 in the 1986–1991 period to 833,400 in the latest 1995–2000 period. One possible explanation for this reduction may be due to the preference of employers to employ the cheaper and readily available foreign workers, both legal and illegal, rather than locals from other parts of the country. Despite the fall in the total volume, the urban/urban migration has managed to register even a slight rise from 513,300 in the first period to 573,700 in the second period. This may be attributed to a huge increase in the pool of urban population from 8,898,600 or 50.7 per cent in 1991 to 14,426,900 or 62.0 per cent in 2000. All the other three types of movements were subjected to a downtrend. Urban/rural migration fell by about half, rural/urban by one-third, and rural/rural by two-thirds.

An innovation introduced in the 1980 Census was the attempt to collect information on the reasons for migration by means of the question, "Why did you move to your present place of residence?"[11] The information collected suffer from certain shortcomings. First, in view of the various constraints in the actual enumeration of respondents in the census, only the principal reason for changing residence was obtained since the migrants have usually moved because of a combination of reasons. Second, the answers were subject to errors arising from the use of proxy respondents, recall biases and *post hoc* rationalisation. Finally, since the answers refer to the reason for moving to the locality of enumeration, the information is only related to the pull-factor, and there is no corresponding information on the push-factor. These limitations should be borne in mind when interpreting the main results summarised in Table 4.8.

The reasons that influenced people to move to their place of residence at the time of the 1980 Census date seemed to vary among the four types of internal migration. Some 32.2 per cent of the rural-urban migrants

TABLE 4.8
Percentage Distribution of Internal Migrants
by Type and Reason, 1980

Reasons	Urban to Urban	Urban to Rural	Rural to Urban	Rural to Rural
Employment	27.1	24.7	32.2	21.5
Rural Development Project	0.5	2.1	0.5	5.6
Education	4.1	1.9	9.5	2.9
Marriage	11.7	13.9	13.4	18.2
Followed Family	40.7	42.9	33.7	41.6
Others	15.9	14.5	10.7	10.2
Total	100.0	100.0	100.0	100.0

moved to the urban centres to take up employment as against the lowest figure of 21.5 per cent for rural-rural migrants. The somewhat high figure of 27.1 per cent for the urban-urban migrants serves to confirm the greater job opportunities in the urban centres. Again, the superior educational facilities in the urban centres as perceived by migrants are manifested in the higher proportion of migrants moving on account of education among the rural-urban migrants with 9.5 per cent and the urban-urban migrants with 4.1 per cent. Only 1.9 per cent of the urban-rural migrants and 2.9 per cent of the rural-rural migrants cited education as the reason for moving residence.

It is obvious the biggest proportion for rural development project reason should be registered by the rural-rural migrants with 5.6 per cent and the second biggest by the urban-rural migrants with 2.1 per cent. More often than not, the rural development projects involved the clearing of virgin jungles for agriculture and housing. The relatively lowest proportion of rural-urban migrants among the four types who moved just to follow the family was obviously due to the higher proportion of single persons among this type of internal migration. By and large, migrants tend to move to the urban centres on account of economic reasons, while those who moved to the rural areas were influenced by family reasons.

Notes

1. Malaysia, *Third Malaysia Plan 1976–1980* (Kuala Lumpur: Government Printer, 1976).
2. Malaysia, *Second Malaysia Plan 1971–1975* (Kuala Lumpur: Government Printer, 1971).
3. Haji Aziz bin Othman, *2000 General Report of the Population and Housing Census* (Kuala Lumpur: Department of Statistics, 2005).
4. A discussion of the various methods is given in United Nations, *Manual VI: Methods of Measuring Internal Migration* (New York: Department of International Economic and Social Affairs, 1970).
5. Saw Swee-Hock, *Estimation of Interstate Migration in Peninsular Malaysia, 1947–1970* (Singapore: Institute of Southeast Asian Studies, 1980).
6. Babara Watson Andaya and Leonard Y. Andaya, *A History of Malaysia* (Honolulu: University of Hawaii Press, 2001).
7. Shaari bin Abdul Rahman, *2000 Population and Housing Census, Migration and Population Distribution* (Kuala Lumpur: Department of Statistics, 2004).
8. E.G. Ravenstein, "The Law of Migration", *Journal of the Royal Statistical Society* (June 1879).
9. R.J. Pryor, "Law of Migraton: The Experience of Malaysia and Other Countries", *Geographica* 5 (1969).
10. Khoo Soo Gim, *1991 General Report of the Population Census*, Volume 1 (Kuala Lumpur: Department of Statistics, 1993).
11. Khoo Teik Huat, *1980 General Report of the Population Census*, Volume 1 (Kuala Lumpur: Department of Statistics, 1983).

5

Ethnic and Religious Patterns

The large inflow of immigrants from China and South Asia during the British colonial period has led to the emergence of a multiracial population that has persisted until today. Since the immigrants brought with them their religious practices different from the Bumiputera's, the population also became multi-religious in character. The close identification of ethnicity with religion reinforced the sharp divide between the different ethnic communities in the country. Some difficulties and challenges have always been encountered in the collection and presentation of statistics on ethnicity and religion, and they will be discussed in their respective sections.

The collection of information on ethnicity has assumed greater significance in recent years since it provides a major impact on the formulation and monitoring of government policies and programmes designed to eliminate the identification of race with economic activities. Undoubtedly, ethnic data compiled from the census would be essential for a fuller understanding of the country's demographics in view of the influence of ethnicity on the various population characteristics. The item pertaining to race has always been included in the population censuses conducted in Malaysia, though some changes in the definition and presentation of the statistics have been introduced over the years.

A better appreciation of the ethnic information requires an explanation of the definition of the different ethnic terminologies used in the population censuses. The definition of *Chinese* has always been quite clear-cut, referring to people of Chinese descent regardless of their country of birth or citizenship. The term *Indians* has not been consistently defined in past censuses, but it is now employed to refer to persons from the Indian subcontinent such as Indians, Pakistanis, Bangladeshis, and Sri Lankans. The definition, also disregarding citizenship or birthplace, makes sense because these people display fairly common social and cultural traits, and hence similar demographic characteristics.

The term *Bumiputeras* was introduced in the pan-Malaysia Censuses to accommodate the emergence of a large variety of indigenous communities after the creation of Malaysia in 1963. The Bumiputera group is now divided into *Malays* and *Other Bumiputeras* in most of the tables presented in the census reports. The latter refers mainly to the *Orang Asli* in West Malaysia and the numerous small indigenous tribes in Sabah and Sarawak. The definition of "Malays" is enshrined in Article 160(2) of the Constitution of Malaysia, which specifies that a Malay is a "person who professed the Muslim religion, habitually speaks the Malay language and conforms to the Malay custom".

The presentation of statistics on ethnic groups in the first two pan-Malaysia censuses is given in terms of the total population, while the figures for the two censuses 1991 and 2000, and the postcensal estimates for 2005 are for Malaysian citizens rather than the combined total for citizens and non-citizens as provided in the earlier censuses.[1] The departure from previous practice was meant to avoid distortion or misrepresentation by taking into account the prevailing situation in Malaysia which had experienced a heavy inflow of migrants in recent years.[2] Restricting ethnic information to citizen population only would hopefully yield more meaningful statistics viewed in terms of government policies and electoral dynamics. It is important to bear in mind that ethnicity can only be studied in the two latest censuses, and post-2000 census estimates, in terms of the citizen population. In fact, the statistics for non-citizen population released in the two latest census reports have not been made available according to quite a number of other variables, certainly not according to ethnicity.

ETHNIC COMPOSITION

The discontinuity in the presentation of official statistics regarding ethnicity forces us to analyse the ethnic composition in two separate periods as shown in Table 5.1 and 5.2. In the first table for 1970 and 1980, the figures are for the total population and not the citizen population, and are given according to the four-group classification. The Malays recorded an enlargement from 5,844,500 in 1970 to 7,782,700 in 1980, an increase of 1,938,200 or 32.9 per cent during the ten-year intercensal period. In sharp contrast, the same period saw the Chinese growing at a very slow pace of 16.5 per cent, bring the population from 3,564,400 in 1970 to 4,167,100 in 1980. An almost similar growth rate, 16.4 per cent, was experienced by the Indians who witnessed their population rise from 943,400 to 1,098,400 during the same period. The above differential rate of increase among the three main ethnic groups has naturally led to a shift in the ethnic composition of the country. The proportion of Malays was raised from 56.0 per cent in 1970 to 59.2 per cent in 1980, while the proportion of Chinese was lowered from 34.2 per cent to 31.7 per cent. The Indians also has their proportion reduced from 9.0 per cent to 8.4 per cent during the same period. It should be mentioned that the 1980 figure for the 'Indians" does not include the Indians in Sarawak; they have been included under "Others". But the number involved is so small that our interpretation of the data shown in the table is still essentially valid.

The postcensal estimates after 2000 prepared by the Department of Statistics have also followed the practice adopted in the last two censuses of making available ethnic information according to citizen population only.[3] The 2005 figures given in Table 5.2 are therefore consistent with those for the two censuses. Another point to bear in mind is that the term "Bumiputera" has been assuming greater prominence in recent years, and it is used to encompass the Malays and other indigenous peoples, especially those in the eastern states of Sabah and Sarawak. It is therefore customary to present the information in two separate categories, the Malays and the other Bumiputeras as shown in Table 5.2.

During the nine-year intercensal period 1991–2000, the number of Malays among the citizen population was raised from 8,521,900 to

TABLE 5.1
Distribution of Total Population by Ethnic Group, 1970–1980

Ethnic Group	1970 ('000)	1980 ('000)	Increase		Percentage	
			Number	%	1970	1980
Malays	5,844.5	7,782.7	1,938.2	32.9	56.0	59.2
Chinese	3,564.4	4,167.1	602.7	16.9	34.2	31.7
Indians	943.4	1,098.4	155.0	16.4	9.0	8.4
Others	87.0	87.9	0.9	1.0	0.8	0.7
Total	10,439.3	13,136.1	2,696.8	25.8	100.0	100.0

TABLE 5.2
Distribution of Citizen Population by Ethnic Group, 1991–2005

Ethnic Group	1991 ('000)	2000 ('000)	2005 ('000)	Increase 1991–2000 Number ('000)	Increase 1991–2000 %	Increase 2000–2005 Number ('000)	Increase 2000–2005 %	Percentage 1991	Percentage 2000	Percentage 2005
Malays	8,521.9	11,680.4	13,190.2	3,158.5	37.1	1,520.0	13.0	50.7	53.4	54.1
Other Bumiputeras	1,778.0	2,567.8	2,870.3	789.8	44.4	302.5	11.8	10.6	11.7	11.8
Chinese	4,623.9	5,691.9	6,154.9	1,068.0	23.1	463.0	8.1	27.5	26.0	25.3
Indians	1,316.1	1,680.1	1,834.8	364.0	27.7	154.7	9.2	7.8	7.7	7.5
Others	572.4	269.7	311.8	-302.7	-52.9	42.1	15.6	3.4	1.2	1.3
Total	16,812.3	21,889.7	24,362.0	5,077.6	30.2	2,472.6	11.3	100.0	100.0	100.0

11,680,400, giving an increase of some 3,158,500 or 37.1 per cent. The same period witnessed a larger increase of 44.4 per cent by the other Bumiputeras, which saw their numbers shooting up from 1,778,000 to well above the two million mark of 2,567,800. The Chinese, on the other hand, grew by a much smaller rate of 23.1 per cent and the Indians fare no better, 27.7 per cent. This pattern of growth among the main ethnic groups continued in the postcensal years 2000–2005, with the Malays growing by 13.0 per cent, the other Bumiputeras by 11.8 per cent, the Chinese by 8.1 per cent and the Indians by 9.2 per cent. The lower level of fertility and the absence of migration inflow from China and the Indian sub-continent were the principal factors responsible for the slower growth rate among the Chinese and the Indians.

One of the major consequences of the differences in the rate of increase among the ethnic groups is reflected in the conspicuous shift in the ethnic composition of the citizen population. The share of the Malays in the citizen population was enlarged from 50.7 per cent in 1991 to 54.1 per cent in 2005, and the other Bumiputeras also saw their share soar from 10.6 per cent to 11.8 per cent. During the same period, the share of the Chinese fell from 27.5 per cent to 25.3 per cent and that of the Indians from 7.8 per cent to 7.7 per cent. Needless to say, these changes in the ethnic composition of the citizen population would have profound political, cultural and economic implications in such a multiracial society like Malaysia. Some segments of the community have expressed their apprehension about their diminishing share of the population, with the Malaysian Chinese Association (MCA) issuing periodic exhortation to Chinese couples to produce more babies.[4] The overbearing dominance of the Bumiputeras is present in almost every facet of the daily life of the people in the country.

REGIONAL ETHNIC COMPOSITION

The data in respect of the ethnic composition of the citizen population in the various parts of the country as compiled in the 2000 Census are presented in Table 5 3. We have decided to use the 2000 Census figures instead of the 2005 postcensal estimates because the latter figures do not provide a breakdown of the Bumiputera population into Malays and Other Bumiputeras. The combined Bumiputera group constituted the majority in all states, except Penang and Kuala Lumpur. The majority status reached the highest level in Trengganu with 96.8 per cent and in

TABLE 5.3

Percentage Distribution of Citizen Population by Ethnic Group, Region and State, 2000

Region/State	Malays	Other Bumiputeras	Chinese	Indians	Others	Total
			Region			
MALAYSIA	53.4	11.7	26.0	7.7	1.2	100.0
West Malaysia	61.0	1.4	27.4	9.5	0.7	100.0
Sabah	15.3	65.3	13.2	0.5	5.8	100.0
Sarawak	23.0	49.8	26.7	0.2	0.2	100.0
			West Malaysian States			
Johore	55.7	1.4	35.4	6.9	0.6	100.0
Kedah	76.4	0.2	14.9	7.1	1.4	100.0
Kelantan	94.2	0.8	3.8	0.3	0.9	100.0
Malacca	62.7	1.1	29.1	6.5	0.6	100.0
Negri Sembilan	56.6	1.3	25.6	16.0	0.5	100.0
Pahang	71.8	5.0	17.7	5.0	0.5	100.0
Penang	42.1	0.3	46.5	10.6	0.4	100.0
Perak	52.4	2.3	32.0	13.0	0.3	100.0
Perlis	85.2	0.3	10.3	1.3	2.9	100.0
Selangor	52.1	1.4	30.7	14.6	1.1	100.0
Trengganu	96.5	0.3	2.8	0.2	0.2	100.0
Kuala Lumpur	42.7	0.9	43.5	11.4	1.5	100.0

Kelantan with 95.0 per cent. Within the Bumiputera group, the Malays dominate all the states in West Malaysia but not in Sabah and Sarawak. In these two states, the Malays comprised only 15.3 per cent and 23.0 per cent respectively. The various indigenous peoples classified as Other Bumiputeras were in fact the majority, with 65.3 per cent in Sabah and 49.8 per cent in Sarawak.

The Chinese have always formed the majority in Penang, but this dominant position has been diminishing over the years. In 2000, the Chinese amounted to 46.5 per cent, just a shade higher than the 42.4 per cent for the Bumiputeras. In Kuala Lumpur, the share of the citizen population taken up by each of these two ethnic groups is almost equal, 43.5 per cent for the Chinese and 43.6 per cent for the Bumiputeras. The other states with sizeable proportion of Chinese are also found along the western coast of Peninsular Malaysia, 35.9 per cent in Johore, 32.0 per cent in Perak and 3C.7 per cent in Selangor.

A somewhat similar pattern of higher proportion in the states sprang along the western part of the Peninsula is exhibited by the Indians, 16.0 per cent in Negri Sembilan, 14.6 per cent in Selangor, 13.0 per cent in Perak, 11.4 per cent in Kuala Lumpur, and 10.3 per cent in Penang. As mentioned earlier, the penetration of these two immigrant communities has been in these western states.

Unlike the pre-eminence of Malays among the Bumiputeras in all the states in West Malaysia, there is a greater variety of sub-groups in Sabah and Sarawak as can be observed in Table 5.4. In 2000 the largest indigenous community in Sabah are the Kadazans/Dusuns whose share of the total citizen population approached 484,800 or 30.3 per cent. Incidentally, in the 1991 Census, the statistics for this group were presented separately into two categories, 217,600 for the Dusuns and 107,500 for the Kadazans. The second largest tribes are the Bajans accounting for 21.1 per cent followed closely by the Malays with 20.2 per cent. The Muruts managed to take up only 5.2 per cent share of the citizen population.

TABLE 5.4

Distribution of Bumiputera Citizen Population in Sabah and Sarawak by Sub-Ethnic Group, 2000

Sub-Ethnic Group	Number	Percentage
Sabah		
Malays	332,471	20.2
Kadazans/Dusuns	484,828	30.3
Bajans	347,193	21.1
Muruts	85,094	5.2
Other Bumiputeras	394,464	24.2
Total	1,601,356	100.0
Sarawak		
Malays	462,270	31.6
Ibans	603,735	41.3
Bidayuhs	166,756	11.4
Melanaus	112,984	7.7
Other Bumiputeras	117,690	8.0
Total	1,463,435	100.0

An entirely different composition of the Bumiputera citizen population is displayed in Sarawak. The Ibans, also known as Sea Dayaks, constituted the biggest tribe totaling some 603,700 or 41.3 per cent. The Malays, living mainly in towns and coastal areas, formed the second largest community with a share of 31.6 per cent. The less important tribes are Bidayahs with 11.4 per cent and the Melanaus with only 7.7 per cent. In the past, these two tribes resided in the riverine and coastal villages, but some of them were later re-settled in the interior.

The figures given in Table 5.4 have not done justice to the much greater number of tribes existing in the two states. The other indigenous tribes not mentioned separately are rather small in number and for practical purposes have been lumped together as *Others*. In Sabah the minority tribes are the Kwijaus, Iranum, Tidong, Rungus, Tambanuo, Dumpas, Paitan, Idahan, Minokok, Kadayan, Bisaya, etc., numbering some 390,000 or 24.2 per cent. The corresponding figures for the *Other Bumiputeras* in Sarawak are not large, only 117,700 or 8.0 per cent. This small group consisted of Bisaya, Kadayan, Kayan, Kenyah, Kelabit and Punan. The colourful variety of the indigenous peoples in the two east Malaysian states has indeed enhanced the greater ethnic diversity in the overall population of Malaysia.

It would be useful to look at the distribution of the citizen population according to urban/rural classification within each ethnic community. Out of a total of 11,680,400 Malays enumerated among the citizen population in 2000, some 6,336,000 or 56.7 per cent were residing in the urban area, while the other 5,344,400 or 43.3 per cent in the rural area. Among the 2,567,800 other Bumiputeras, a smaller proportion of 34.0 per cent stayed in the urban area as against the 66.0 per cent in the rural area. Most of them are the indigenous peoples located in the remote interior regions of Sabah and Sarawak. The Chinese and the Indians continued to be found mainly in the towns, their respective proportions of urban dwellers reaching 85.9 per cent and 79.7 per cent.

Another way of looking at the data laid out in Table 5.5 is to examine separately the urban and rural population in terms of the main ethnic groups. Out of a total of 13,610,400 staying in the urban area, some 46.6 per cent were Malays, 6.4 per cent other Bumiputeras, 35.9 per cent Chinese and 9.8 per cent Indians. This is quite different from the ethnic composition of the population residing in the rural area of the country. As high as 64.6 per cent were Malays and 20.5 per cent were other Bumiputeras. In comparison, the Chinese accounted for only 9.7 per cent, and the Indians even less, 4.1 per cent. One of the implications of this pattern of ethnic composition in the rural area is that only candidates from Bumiputera-based parties would stand a good chance of garnering the rural votes.

RELIGIOUS COMPOSITION

Religious differences in Malaysia have a strong tendency to follow ethnic and cultural identities of the people, and have reinforced the great divide among them in almost every aspect of their daily life. The recent resurgence of religious fervour has propelled religion into the forefront

TABLE 5.5
Distribution of Citizen Population by
Ethnic Group and Urban/Rural Area, 2000

Ethnic Group	Urban	Rural	Total
	Number		
Malays	6,335,994	5,344,427	11,680,421
Other Bumiputeras	874,139	1,693,619	2,567,758
Chinese	4,891,752	800,156	5,691,908
Indians	1,338,510	341,622	1,680,132
Others	170,021	99,676	269,697
Total	13,610,416	8,279,500	21,889,916
	Percentage		
Malays	46.6	64.6	53.4
Other Bumiputeras	6.4	20.5	11.7
Chinese	35.9	9.7	26.0
Indians	9.8	4.1	7.7
Others	1.2	1.2	1.2
Total	100.0	100.0	100.0
	Percentage		
Malays	56.7	43.3	100.0
Other Bumiputeras	34.0	66.0	100.0
Chinese	85.9	14.1	100.0
Indians	79.7	20.3	100.0
Others	63.0	37.0	100.0
Total	62.2	37.8	100.0

as the key parameter determining the political and racial harmony of the nation.[5] An evaluation of the religious affiliations of the people is somewhat handicapped by the traditional difficulties encountered in the collection of information on religion, a process involving a wide range of personal beliefs and practices. This should be taken into consideration when attempting to interpret the census statistics concerning religion.

The different religions professed by the people in the country have been quite established, particularly among the Muslims who are prohibited by Islamic laws to convert to another religion or to renounce Islam. Whatever changes in religious affiliations that have occurred in the past would in the main be a reflection of the changing ethnic composition discussed earlier. In looking at this linkage, we should be mindful of the difference in the census statistics for religion and ethnicity. Whilst the ethnic statistics refer to the citizen population only, the statistics for religion are made available for the total population as well as for the two sub-components, citizens and non-citizens. In Table 5.6 the data refers to the religious affiliations of the total population in the last three censuses. Similar figures for 1970 are not available because the item on religion was not included in the census conducted in this year.

It is clear that the predominant religion in the country is Islam, which has enhanced in importance from around 52.9 per cent in 1980 to 60.8 per cent in 2000 following the rise in Malay population. Except for Buddhism and Christianity, the relative importance of the other religions has been declining over the years. A slight rise in the proportion from 17.3 per cent to 18.9 per cent was recorded by Buddhism, but the most recent proportion is still a very poor second as compared to the Muslim proportion. One notable feature refers to the steep rise in the number of Christians from 843,000 to 2,023,500 between 1980 and 2000, resulting in their share moving up from 6.4 per cent to 9.1 per cent. Since Muslims almost never convert to Christianity, the rising importance of Christianity can only be brought about by Chinese, Indians and other minority communities converting to this religion. Christianity has even overtaken Hinduism as the third largest religion professed by the peoples of Malaysia.

The overall rise in the proportion of persons declaring Buddhism as their religion should perhaps be examined further in relation to the sharp drop in the proportion of persons following Confucianism, Taoism and other traditional Chinese religions. The statistics on this mixture of ill-defined Chinese religions are always difficult to collect in the population

TABLE 5.6

Distribution of Population by Religion, 1980–2000

Religion	1980	1992	2000
	Number ('000)		
Islam	6,918.3	10,257.2	13,498.0
Buddhism	2,265.5	3,222.1	4,197.1
Confucianism/Taoism/Others	1,518.7	928.0	579.4
Hinduism	920.4	1,112.3	1,380.4
Christianity	843.0	1,412.3	2,023.5
Tribal/Folk Religions	259.5	206.0	179.9
Others	69.8	82.6	83.8
No Religion/Unknown	275.3	277.7	256.0
Total	13,070.4	17,498.1	22,198.1
	Percentage		
Islam	52.9	58.6	60.8
Buddhism	17.3	18.4	18.9
Confucianism/Taoism/Others	11.6	5.3	2.6
Hinduism	7.0	6.4	6.2
Christianity	6.4	8.1	9.1
Tribal/Folk Religions	2.0	1.2	0.8
Others	0.5	0.5	0.4
No Religion/Unknown	2.1	1.6	1.2
Total	100.0	100.0	100.0

censuses because the loose character of these traditional religions is not amenable to precise identification in the field enumeration. We know that the Chinese population has continued to increase in the last two decades, and yet the number professing this mixture of traditional religions has fallen steeply from 1,518,700 in 1980 to 579,400 in 2000, with the corresponding proportion tumbling from 11.6 per cent to 2.6 per cent. This strongly suggests that there was a shift from this group of traditional religions to Buddhism among the Chinese respondents. In fact, the combined proportion for these two religious groups in Table 5.6 has been reduced from 28.9 per cent to 21.5 per cent, a trend quite consonant with the fall in the share of the Chinese in the total population of Malaysia.

RELIGIOUS COMPOSITION OF ETHNIC GROUPS

A greater insight into the religious character of the plural society can be derived by studying the cross-classification of religion with ethnicity. However, this can only be accomplished in terms of the citizen population only since the non-citizen population has not been tabulated according to ethnicity in the 2000 Census reports. The data presented in Table 5.7 refer to the citizen population only. Despite this limitation, the close association of ethnicity along religious affiliations is quite apparent. The best example is of course the Malays, all of whom profess the Islamic faith as required by law. They are primarily Sunni Muslims practising the Islam Shafe school of thought.

The above link is also perceptible among the Chinese and Indians, though not as rigid as in the case of the Malays. The dominant religion among the Indians in the citizen population has always been Hinduism, accounting for 84.1 per cent in 2000. The second most important religion professed by them is Christianity (7.8 per cent) and the third is Islam (4.1 per cent). Most of the Indian Muslims are Pakistanis and Bangladeshis. Though not prohibited by law, very few Chinese care to convert to the Islamic faith. They practise mainly Buddhism (76.0 per cent), Confucianism, Taoism and other traditional religions (10.6 per cent) and Christianity (9.5 per cent).

The other Bumiputera community has contributed not only a greater variety to the ethnic structure of the country, but also a wide range of religious affiliations. As compared to the above three ethnic groups, the other Bumiputera communities are the only people with the majority professing to be Christians (49.7 per cent). The Muslims (40.8 per cent) occupy second position. The other interesting feature is that they have a sizeable proportion practising some form of tribal and folk religions.

It may be recalled that the non-citizen population has not been tabulated according to ethnicity in the 2000 Census report, but the report has made available statistics on the religious affiliation of this group of the population. A scrutiny of the statistics may give us some insight into the ethnic composition of this group of mainly foreigners. Out of the total non-citizen population of 1,384,880 in 2000, the number professing to follow the Islamic faith amounted to the high of 1,136,000 or 82.0 per cent. This may be taken to confirm the common knowledge that the foreigners, who entered Malaysia, whether legally or not, came principally from Indonesia and to a lesser extent from Bangladesh and Pakistan. The extremely low level of Buddhists (3.5 per cent) and Hindus

TABLE 5.7

Distribution of Citizen Population by Religion and Ethnic Group, 2000

Religion	Malays	Other Bumiputeras	Chinese	Indians	Others	Total	Non-Citizens
			Number ('000)				
Islam	11,680.4	932.0	57.2	69.0	174.8	12,913.4	1,136.0
Buddhism	—	21.6	4,325.0	20.1	52.4	4,419.0	48.5
Confucianism/ Taoism/Others	—	3.1	605.6	1.2	0.7	610.7	4.4
Hinduism	—	2.2	16.1	1,412.7	2.3	1,433.3	24.6
Christianity	—	1,275.0	539.6	130.4	35.5	1,980.4	145.8
Tribal/Folk Religion	—	186.4	7.9	0.9	0.7	195.3	0.6
Others	—	35.6	12.2	35.6	1.0	84.5	4.0
No Religion	—	93.8	88.9	0.8	1.3	184.7	9.6
Unknown	—	18.2	39.5	9.3	1.7	68.6	11.4
Total	11,680.4	2,567.8	5,691.9	1,680.1	269.7	21,889.9	1,384.9
			Percentage				
Islam	100.0	40.8	1.0	4.1	64.8	60.4	82.0
Buddhism	—	0.8	76.0	1.2	19.4	19.2	3.5
Confucianism/ Taoism/Others	—	0.1	10.6	0.7	0.2	2.6	0.3
Hinduism	—	0.1	0.3	84.1	2.6	6.3	1.8
Christianity	—	49.7	9.5	7.8	13.2	9.1	10.5
Tribal/Folk Religion	—	7.2	0.1	0.1	0.2	0.8	0.0
Others	—	1.4	0.2	2.1	0.4	0.4	0.3
No Religion	—	3.7	1.6	0.1	0.5	0.8	0.7
Unknown	—	0.7	0.7	0.6	0.6	0.3	0.8
Total	100.0	100.0	100.0	100.0	100.0	100.0	100.0

(1.8 per cent) surely point to the negligible inflow of Chinese and Indian immigrants.

REGIONAL RELIGIOUS COMPOSITION

The dominant role exerted by religion in the regional politics of the country has been shaped by the religious affiliation of the people in the different states. In analysing the information provided in Table 5.8, we should bear in mind that the ethnic composition discussed earlier has a close association with the data given in the table. The dominance of Islam is obvious in Trengganu (96.9 per cent), Kelantan (94.5 per cent), Perlis (85.4 per cent) and Kedah (76.9 per cent). In these states, the battle for the Muslim votes during the elections has always been very intense between the Pan-Islamic Party (PAS) and the United Malay Organisation (UMNO), the main party in Barisan Nasional.

Buddhism, practised mainly by the Chinese and to some extent by the other minority communities, does not appear to assume such an important role in the various states. The highest proportion of Buddhism practised in these states managed to attain only 33.6 per cent in Penang and also the high of 34.5 per cent in Kuala Lumpur. This is clearly related to the presence of sizeable Chinese population in these two areas. The other states where a fair proportion of their population professed to practise Buddhism are Johore (27.3 per cent), Selangor (24.4 per cent), Malacca (24.2 per cent) and Perak (24.0 per cent). These are states along the west coast of the Peninsula where a substantial number of Chinese reside.

The other religions are professed to a much smaller extent by the population in the various states except Sabah and Sarawak. Hinduism, the principal religion of Indians, was adhered to by 13.9 per cent in Negri Sembilan, 12.1 per cent in Selangor, and 11.1 per cent in Perak. More interesting is Christianity being practised by the majority of people in Sarawak, 42.4 per cent as against the 31.7 per cent for Islam. Even in Sabah, a fair proportion of the people practised Christianity, about one-fourth as compared to two-thirds for Islam. In these two eastern states the Christian missionaries were fairly successful in persuading the predominantly rural indigenous peoples to forsake their folk religion for Christianity. Christianity is practised by a negligible proportion of the population, 0.2 to 4.3 per cent, in each of the West Malaysian states. As to be expected, a higher proportion of 5.6 per cent prevails in Kuala Lumpur where most of the Christian expatriates reside and work in the

TABLE 5.8

Percentage Distribution of Population by Religion and State, 2000

Region/State	Islam	Buddhism	Confucianism/ Taoism/Others	Hinduism	Christianity	Tribal/ Folk Religion	Others	No Religion/ Unknown	Total
Johore	60.8	27.3	3.1	5.8	2.0	0.2	0.2	0.7	100.0
Kedah	77.5	13.2	2.0	6.4	0.8	0.0	0.1	0.1	100.0
Kelantan	95.0	3.9	0.1	0.2	0.2	0.5	0.0	0.0	100.0
Malacca	64.4	24.2	1.5	5.6	3.7	0.0	0.2	0.4	100.0
Negri Sembilan	58.2	20.6	3.1	13.9	2.7	0.6	0.3	0.5	100.0
Pahang	74.5	13.6	2.5	4.4	1.2	2.9	0.2	0.8	100.0
Penang	44.5	33.6	8.7	8.7	3.6	0.0	0.3	0.6	100.0
Perak	53.9	24.0	5.9	11.1	3.1	0.6	0.6	0.9	100.0
Perlis	86.2	10.7	1.4	1.0	0.5	0.0	0.1	0.1	100.0
Sabah	63.4	6.5	0.4	0.1	28.0	0.0	0.3	1.3	100.0
Sarawak	31.7	11.8	2.5	0.1	42.4	5.2	1.3	4.8	100.0
Selangor	55.8	24.4	2.0	12.1	4.2	0.2	0.4	0.9	100.0
Trengganu	96.9	2.5	0.1	0.2	0.3	0.0	0.0	0.1	100.0
Kuala Lumpur	46.0	34.5	2.7	8.4	5.5	0.0	0.7	2.2	100.0

private corporations. In reality, the multi-religious character of the population does not prevail in every part of the country, certainly not in the northern and eastern states of the Peninsula.

The close correlation between religion and ethnicity naturally leads to marked variations in the religious pattern prevailing in the urban and rural areas with completely different ethnic composition. This aspect of the religions professed by the people is presented in Table 5.9 showing the distribution of the religious affiliations of the inhabitants in the urban and rural areas. Clearly, Islam was the major religion practised in the urban area where some 53.3 per cent were Muslims, but in the rural area the position was more dominant as 72.5 per cent belonged to the same religion. In this, lies the intense competition between UMNO and PAS for the votes of the rural folks during state and Federal elections.

The fairly high proportion (26.3 per cent) in the urban area and the very low proportion (6.9 per cent) in the rural area practising Buddhism is of course associated with the Chinese being predominantly urban dwellers. Interestingly, in the rural area Buddhism was even overtaken by Christianity (11.5 per cent) as the second most popular religion due to the conspicuous proportion of rural folks in the two eastern states professing the latter religion. In fact, this proportion of Christianity was higher than that registered in the urban area.

The complex diversity of the population has not only added enduring richness to the social and cultural mosaic of the nation, but has engendered

TABLE 5.9
Percentage Distribution of Population by Religion and Urban/Rural Area, 2000

Religion	Urban	Rural
Islam	53.3	72.9
Buddhism	26.3	6.9
Confucianism and other Chinese Religions	3.2	1.7
Hinduism	7.9	3.5
Christianity	7.6	11.5
Tribal/Folk	0.1	1.9
Others	0.4	0.4
No Religion/Unknown	1.1	1.2
Total	100.0	100.0

some difficulties and challenges in the political and economic life of the people. Race and religion have always been linked in Malaysian politics as reflected in times of election and subsequent formation of government at the state and Federal levels.[6] The paramount consideration is underlined by the usual practice of accommodating the competing interests of the various component parties in Barisan Nasional, but maintaining Malay dominance. Islam has recently become a major factor in Malaysian politics since the emergence of the Pan-Islamic Party (PAS), propagating its brand of radical Islamic teachings and practices that appeal to certain segments of the Malay electorate.

The entrenched ethnicity of the population has been a central focus in the formulation of government policies in implementing the New Economic Policy (NEP) up to 1991, and thereafter, the National Development Policy (NDP). The underlying influence of ethnicity is quite pervasive in almost all aspect of government programmes and action, especially in the field of education, workforce, business, land ownership, and rural development.[7] The overriding objective of these policies as advocated by the government is the creation of national unity through the eradication of racial inequality in the social and economic advancement of the people.

Notes

1. Khoo Teik Huat, *1980 General Report on the Population Census*, Volume 1 (Kuala Lumpur: Department of Statistics, 1983).
2. Haji Aziz bin Othman, *2000 General Report of the Population and Housing Census* (Kuala Lumpur: Department of Statistics, 2005).
3. Department of Statistics, *Monthly Statistical Bulletin, Malaysia*, April 2006 (Kuala Lumpur: Department of Statistics, 2006).
4. "Chinese Clan Offers Reward for Having More Babies", *Sunday Times*, 14 July 2002; "MCA Plays Cupid", *Straits Times*, 14 August 2001 and "Declining Birth Rate Worries Chinese Groups", *Straits Times*, 7 May 2001.
5. Terence Chong, "The Emerging Politics of Islam Hadhari" in *Malaysia: Recent Trends and Challenges*, edited by Saw Swee-Hock and K. Kesavapany (Singapore: Institute of Southeast Asian Studies, 2005).
6. Teo Kah Leong, "Race the Key to Understanding Malaysian Politics", *Straits Times*, 15 August 2003.
7. Saw Swee-Hock, "Population Trends and Patterns in Multiracial Malaysia" in *Malaysia: Recent Trends and Challenges*, edited by Saw Swee-Hock and K. Kesavapany (Singapore: Institute of Southeast Asian Studies, 2005).

6

Population Structure

In this chapter we will examine the structure of the population in terms of sex composition, age structure, educational attainment and citizenship pattern. The structure of the population has evolved over many decades in accordance with not only demographic determinants like migration, mortality and fertility, but also social and economic forces. These variables have exerted their influence in different ways and in varying degrees on each aspect of the population structure. In Malaysia international migration has left its pervasive and permanent imprint on many facets of the population. The two important topics concerning ethnic composition and religious pattern have already been examined in the previous chapter.

SEX COMPOSITION

In a closed population unaffected by migration, the sex composition is determined by the proportion of boys and girls at birth, but this is counter-balanced by males being subject to higher mortality so that the eventual sex ratio of the general population is very near normal with fairly even numbers between the two sexes. However, in a country where migration of predominantly males has been a major force of population growth, we can expect the sex ratio to deviate from the normal pattern. This is true in the case of Malaysia where predominantly male migration has always been significant, resulting in more males than females in the population. However, in the course of time a slow movement towards a more balanced sex ratio has taken place, first as the proportion of female immigrants increased, then as the volume of natural increase became larger, and latterly as the flow of migration diminished.

The distribution of the population by sex and the computed sex ratio defined as the number of males per thousand females are presented in Table 6.1. During the first wave of migration before World War II, the male migrant workers had no intention of settling in the country, and hence they left their families in their own country. The extremely uneven sex ratio commenced to improve after the war when the previous large-scale migration ceased but this improvement took a very long time.[1] This is the explanation for the population in 1970 to continue to have more males than females, 5,266,100 and 5,173,300, yielding a sex ratio of 1,018 males per 1,000 males.

As natural increase continued to be the principal factor of population growth in the 1970s, the sex ratio was further improved to 1,006. Thereafter, the revival of migration from the Southeast Asian region led to a reversal, and the sex ratio started to worsen again to 1,022 in 1991 until it reached 1,037 in 2005. Confirmation of the influence of migration on the sex ratio is provided by similar figures for the local-born and foreign-born population as well for the citizen population and non-citizen population. The sex ratio in 2000 was 1,029 for the citizen population and 1,221 for the non-citizen population. Again, the local-born population had a sex ratio of 1,019, in 2000, while the figure for the foreign-born population was 1,190.

For a more detailed explanation of the impact of migrant workers on the sex composition of the overall population, we will turn to the information given in Table 6.2. The link in these figures subdivided into citizens and non-citizens lies in the latter group being dominated by foreigners belonging to the male sex. This is clearly reflected in the more uneven sex ratio displayed by the non-citizen than the citizen population in every one of the five-age groups. In fact, the most uneven ratio was

TABLE 6.1
Distribution of Population by Sex, 1970–2005

Year	Male	Female	Sex Ratio
1970	5,266,100	5,173,300	1,018
1980	6,588,100	6,547,300	1,006
1991	8,876,829	8,686,591	1,022
2000	11,853,432	11,421,258	1,032
2005	13,302,803	12,824,900	1,037

TABLE 6.2
Distribution of Population by Citizenship, Broad Age Group and Sex, 2000

Age Group	Citizens			Non-Citizens		
	Male	Female	Sex Ratio	Male	Female	Sex Ratio
0–4	1,290,176	1,214,017	1,063	57,457	51,094	1,125
5–14	2,560,777	2,423,050	1,057	80,555	73,922	1,090
15–29	2,910,972	2,898,211	1,004	308,415	257,648	1,197
30–59	3,638,984	3,542,228	1,027	312,972	202,547	1,505
60 & Over	672,169	739,332	909	20,955	19,209	1,091
Total	11,073,078	10,816,838	1,024	780,354	604,420	1,291

portrayed by the working-age group 30–59 with 1,505 males per thousand females, and the next uneven ratio by the younger working-age group 15–29 with 1,197. The other interesting feature of the table refers to the sex ratio of 909 for the oldest age group aged 60 and over among the citizen population, caused by the men being exposed to higher mortality than the women at the old ages. The overall sex ratio was naturally more even for the citizen population (1,024) than for the non-citizen population (1,291). This distinctive feature has persisted in 2005 when the two respective overall sex ratio stood at 1,023 and 1,260.[2]

The sex composition of the main ethnic groups can only be analysed in terms of the citizen population because the postcensal estimates for ethnic groups in 2005, as in the 2000 Census, are only available for the citizen population but not for the non-citizen component.[3] The data for the sex ratio of the ethnic groups within the citizen population are given in Table 6.3. The sex ratio was not affected by the recent inflow of migrant workers, but it may still be distorted by male dominated immigration before World War II. This is underlined by the somewhat uneven sex ratio of 1,045 males per thousand females for the Chinese, caused by predominantly male immigrants in the past. It should also be pointed out that the inflow of Chinese from China after the war has been non-existent, or at most negligible. The sex ratio of 996 for the Indians can probably be attributed to their male immigrants eventually returning to South Asia rather than settling down in the country and becoming citizens.

TABLE 6.3
Distribution of Citizen Population by
Sex and Ethnic Group, 2005

Ethnic Group	Male	Female	Sex Ratio
Malays	6,650,600	6,539,600	1,017
Other Bumiputeras	1,449,000	1,421,300	1,019
Chinese	3,144,500	3,010,400	1,045
Indians	916,800	918,000	996
Others	157,400	154,400	1,016

AGE STRUCTURE

In studying the population structure of a country, it would be instructive to examine the age distribution in view of its influence on the amount of labour available, the extent and type of dependency burden, the supply of marriage partners, and the volume of annual births and deaths. In a closed population devoid of any migration, the age distribution is determined mainly by fertility and to a lesser extent by mortality. In such a case the age structure would resemble the shape of a pyramid, with the largest number of the youngest age group at the base, and tapering off upwards with the advance of age as mortality takes its toll. If the population is not a closed one, this normal shape of age distribution will be distorted by migration, the extent of which will depend on the size and type of migrational flows.

The evolution of the age structure over the last thirty-five years is depicted in Table 6.4 in terms of five broad age groups. Two general features stand out clearly. First, as a result of sustained population growth the number in every age group recorded an increase, though at varying speed, over the years. Second, the population structure experienced a gradual but continuous shift from a young one to a relatively older one as evidenced by the changes in the proportionate distribution among the age groups.

The proportion in the youngest age group 0–4 was reduced from 15.8 per cent in 1970 to 11.7 per cent in 2005 and continued to fall throughout the period. For essentially the same reason, the proportion in the schooling age group 5–14 was reduced steadily from 29.1 per cent to 20.9 per cent at the end of the period. The third age group 15–29 constitutes the important and active segment of the population viewed

TABLE 6.4
Distribution of Population by Broad Age Group, 1970–2005

Age Group	1970	1980	1991	2000	2005
	Number ('000)				
0–4	1,651.4	1,779.6	2,234.4	2,612.7	3,054.9
5–14	3,033.1	3,416.3	4,204.5	5,138.3	5,470.3
15–29	2,632.0	3,807.0	4,850.2	6,375.3	6,996.8
30–59	2,576.9	3,388.0	5,242.0	7,696.7	8,874.6
60 & Over	546.0	745.2	1,032.3	1,451.7	1,731.1
Total	10,439.4	13,136.1	17,563.4	23,274.7	26,127.7
	Percentage				
0–4	15.8	13.5	12.7	11.2	11.7
5–14	29.1	26.0	23.9	22.1	20.9
15–29	25.2	29.0	27.6	27.4	26.8
30–59	24.7	25.8	29.8	33.1	34.0
60 & Over	5.2	5.7	5.9	6.2	6.6
Total	100.0	100.0	100.0	100.0	100.0

in terms of employment and reproductive behaviour. The number in this age group was only slightly affected by the recent fertility decline but very much so by the addition of migrant workers. This accounts for the initial rise in the proportion from 25.2 per cent in 1970 to 29.0 per cent in 1980 and the subsequent fall to 26.8 in 2005.

The 30–59 age group composed of the more mature adults of working age and mostly past the prime of their reproductive life. The proportion in this group was boosted not only by the high fertility prevailing up to the 1970s but also by the enormous inflow of migrant workers in recent years. Indeed, the proportion was lifted significantly from 24.7 per cent in 1970 to 34.0 per cent in 2005. A very clear trend can also be observed in the last age group 60 and over, the proportion being raised from 5.2 per cent to 6.6 per cent during the same period. It would appear that the population has commenced to undergo the process of ageing.

The evaluation of the age structure of a population over a long period of time can be examined in terms of an age pyramid which presents the age statistics in a diagrammatic form. In Figure 6.1 are presented the age pyramid for the four censuses and the 2005 postcensal estimates.

FIGURE 6.1
Age Pyramids, 1970–2005

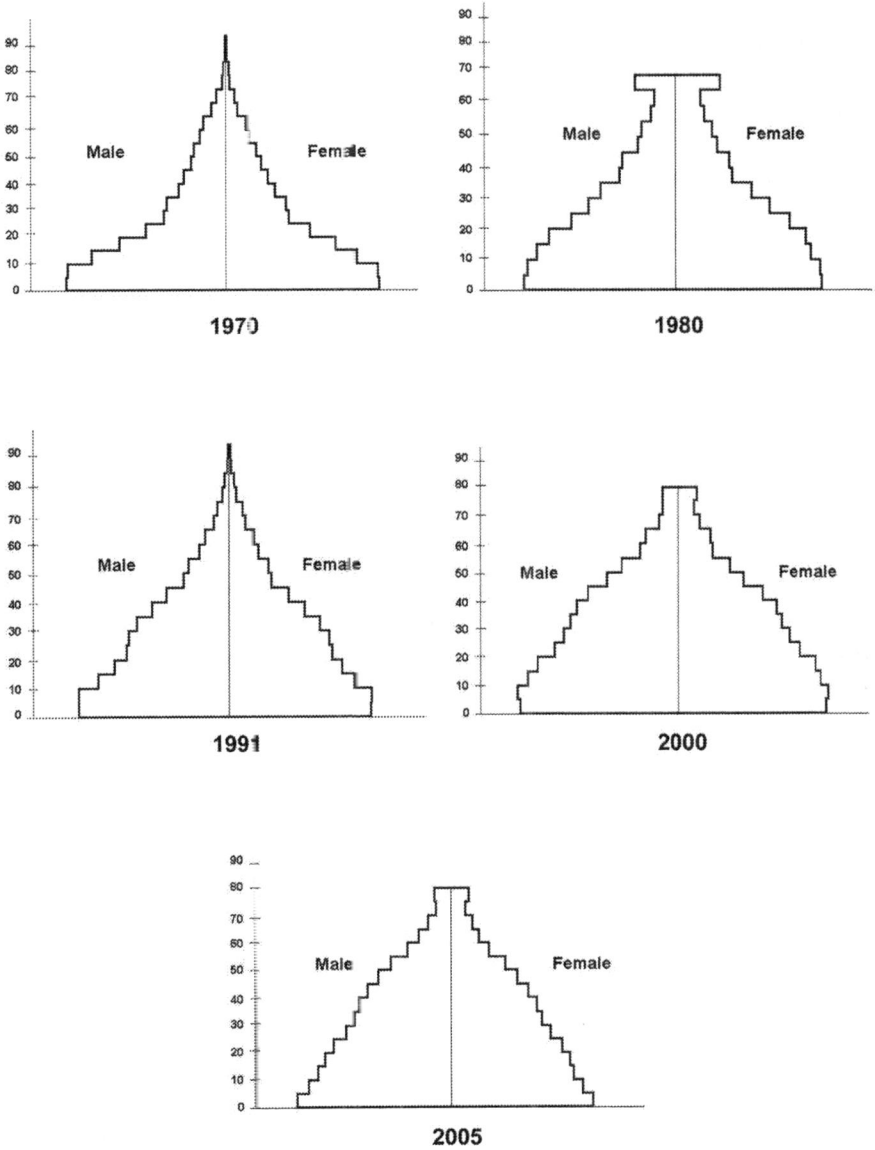

1970

1980

1991

2000

2005

The data laid out in Table 6.4 have been presented in such a manner that they can be utilised to provide an idea of the dependency burden. As a rough guideline, the numbers of persons in the two age groups 15 to 59 may be taken to represent the working population, while those in the age group 0–14 the young dependents and those aged 60 and over the old dependents. This provides only an approximate measure of the relationship between those persons who bear the responsibility to support in society and those who depend on them following their upbringing, education and old age support. It is of course merely an age-based classification and is not directly related to whether the persons are actually in school, at work or in retirement.

Bearing in mind the above limitation, we see that in 1970 about half the population were entrusted with the responsibility of supporting the other half made up of primarily young dependents and some old dependents. The dependency ratio, defined as the number of children below age 15 and old persons aged 60 and over per 100 persons aged 15 to 59, stood at 50 in 1970, and decreased over the years to touch 40 in 2005. This tendency seems to suggest that a smaller dependency burden was being borne by the working persons, but most of the migrant workers have been contributing towards the upkeep of their families left behind in their own country. This is also reflected in similar data for the population divided into citizens and non-citizens, the former with a dependency ratio of 41 as compared to only 22 for the latter in 2000. The other noteworthy feature refers to the pronounced reduction in the

FIGURE 6.2

Age Pyramids of Citizen and Non-Citizen Population, 2000

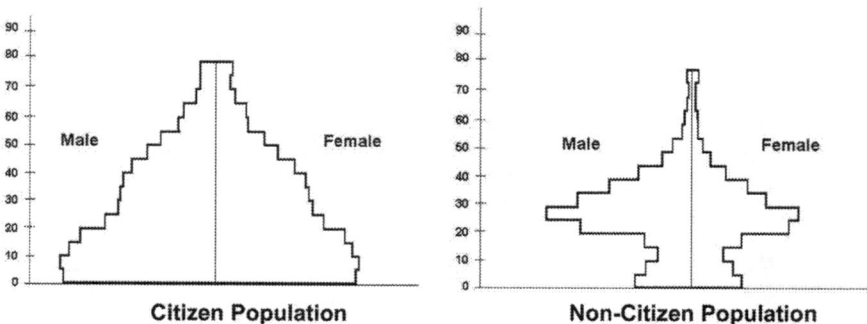

Citizen Population   Non-Citizen Population

proportion of young dependents from 44.9 per cent in 1970 to 32.6 per cent in 2005 as against the slight rise in the proportion of old dependents from 5.2 per cent of 6.6 per cent. The old dependency burden is expected to become heavier as the ageing of the population continues in the years ahead.

A comparison of the age composition of the main ethnic groups within the citizen population in 2000 is presented in Table 6.5. Since these figures have excluded the non-citizen population consisting mainly persons of working ages, they are not in any way affected by the recent inflow of migrants. Natural increase has been the main factor determining the shape of the age structure. There was a smaller proportion of the population in the two young age groups, 8.4 per cent in the 0–4 group and 17.8 per cent in the 5–14 group, among the Chinese. The explanation lies in the much lower fertility experienced by the Chinese prior to 2005, which has also been the same reason for the Chinese recording the highest proportion of 8.8 per cent in the oldest age group 60 and over.

TABLE 6.5
Distribution of Citizen Population by Broad Age Group and Ethnic Group, 2000

Age Group	Malays	Other Bumiputeras	Chinese	Indians	Others
		Number ('000)			
0–4	1,473.7	343.1	476.8	169.5	41.0
5–14	2,908.0	649.9	1,012.4	339.4	74.1
15–29	3,103.9	717.1	1,450.5	469.4	68.3
30–59	3,520.9	727.5	2,251.2	607.9	46.1
60 & Over	673.9	130.2	501.0	93.9	40.2
Total	11,680.4	2,557.8	5,691.9	1,680.1	269.7
		Percentage			
0–4	12.6	13.4	8.4	10.1	15.2
5–14	24.9	25.3	17.8	20.2	27.5
15–29	26.6	27.9	25.5	27.9	25.3
30–59	30.1	28.3	39.5	36.2	17.1
60 & Over	5.8	5.1	8.8	5.6	14.9
Total	100.0	100.0	100.0	100.0	100.0

FIGURE 6.3

Age Pyramids of Ethnic Citizen Population, 2000

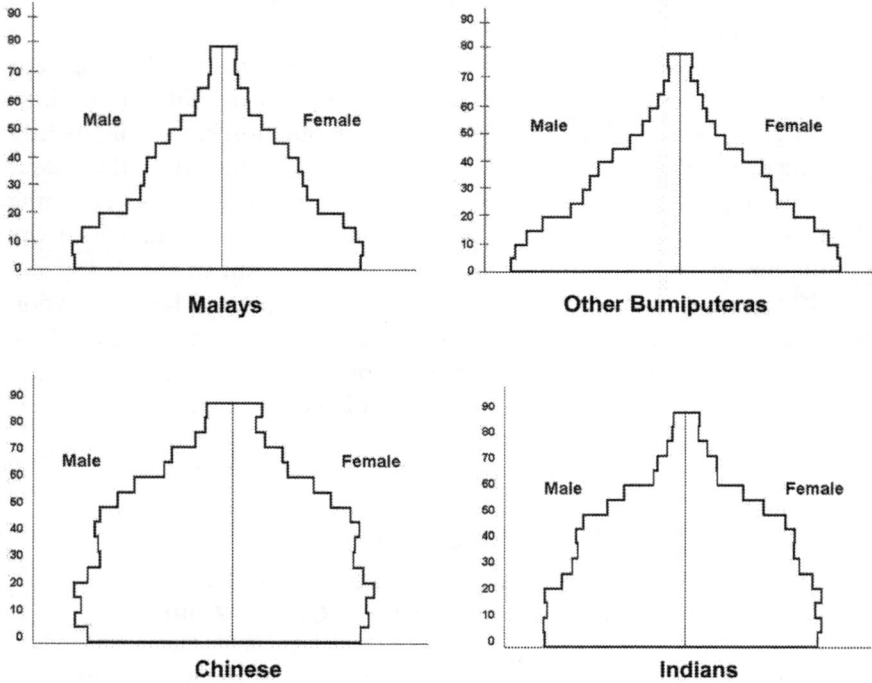

Malays

Other Bumiputeras

Chinese

Indians

This ageing of the Chinese population, according to demographic theory, is due to a decline in fertility rather than mortality in the past.[4]

The Malays and the other Bumiputeras have been experiencing a higher level of fertility, which has resulted in a relatively younger population. The higher proportion in the two young age groups amounted to 12.6 per cent and 24.9 per cent for the Malays and 13.4 per cent and 25.3 per cent for the other Bumiputeras. The proportion at the upper end at age 60 and even stood at 5.8 and 5.1 respectively for these two sub-ethnic groups. These differences among the main ethnic groups within the citizen population are expected to continue to prevail in the future.

EDUCATIONAL ATTAINMENT

Information on educational attainment collected in the four pan-Malaysia Censuses refer to the highest level of education attained. All persons aged 6 and over who had ever attended school were asked to state the highest level of schooling, which they had completed. For the younger respondents who were still schooling at the time of the census, they were categorised according to the level they were currently in on the assumption that they would have completed that level by the end of the school or academic year.[5]

In the census the particulars on educational attainment were collected at each level in primary, secondary, post-secondary and university. However, for the purpose of our analysis, the data on educational attainment have been classified into three broad levels, primary, secondary and tertiary. The primary level includes Standard 1 to Standard 6, while the secondary level includes Form 1 to Form 6 and also secondary Technical and Vocational schooling. Tertiary level is defined to include education in Form 6, polytechnics, colleges and universities. Table 6.6 provides an insight into the changes in educational attainment in the last three decades according to the above categories of education.

Apart from those who had ever attended an educational institution and categorised accordingly. there were those who had never received any education at all, also shown in Table 6.6. Out of a total of 8,682,900

TABLE 6.6
Distribution of Population Aged 6 and Over by
Educational Attainment, 1970–2000

Educational Attainment	1970	1980	1991	2000
	Number ('000)			
Primary	4,393.5	4,966.7	5,760.5	6,147.3
Secondary	1,358.0	3,162.2	5,603.9	8,555.9
Tertiary	84.1	302.9	960.2	1,903.5
Never Attended School	2,847.3	2,500.7	2,326.6	1,782.7
Unknown	0.0	1.0	54.1	482.9
Total	8,682.9	10,932.6	14,705.3	18,872.3
	Percentage			
Primary	50.6	45.4	39.2	32.6
Secondary	15.6	28.9	38.1	45.3
Tertiary	1.0	2.8	6.5	10.1
Never Attended School	32.8	22.9	15.8	9.4
Unknown	0.0	0.0	0.4	2.6
Total	100.0	100.0	100.0	100.0

aged 6 and over in 1970, some 2,847,300 or 32.8 per cent had never received any education. A remarkable improvement occurred over the years, with proportion never attended school being lowered to 22.9 per cent in 1980, 15.8 per cent in 1991, and 9.4 per cent in 2000. This spread of education among the general population may be attributed to the emphasis placed on the development of education in the various Malaysia Plans.

In addition to the rapid spread of universal education, there was a perceptible swift towards a higher level of educational attainment among those who had ever attended school. The number with attainment at primary level rose from 4,393,500 in 1970 to 6,147,300 in 2000, an increase of 39.9 per cent. In sharp contrast, those with attainment at secondary level was enlarged by more than five-fold, bringing the number from only 1,358,000 to 8,555,900 during the thirty-year period. The tertiary level recorded somewhat less progress, the number being raised by slightly more than two-fold. This differential growth led to major changes in the proportions among these broad categories of educational attainment. The proportion with primary education was lowered from 50.6 per cent in 1970 to 32.6 per cent in 2000, as against the rise from 15.6 per cent to 45.3 per cent for secondary education and from 1.0 per cent to 10.1 per cent for tertiary education. During the period, there were greater opportunities for Malaysians to acquire education following the expansion of universities in the public and private sectors.

Education has always been one of the major contentious issues in multiracial Malaysia viewed in terms of the language of instruction and the availability of places for the different ethnic groups in schools and particularly universities.[6] Comprehensive statistics on the various aspects of education have been collected and published in the census reports. The latest position concerning the educational attainment of the main ethnic groups as shown in the 2000 Census is depicted in Table 6.7. A general feature underlined by the figures refers the extremely high proportion of Other Bumiputeras (21.0 per cent) who had never received any education as against the low of 6.4 per cent for the Malays, 7.3 per cent for the Chinese and 6.7 per cent for the Indians. Most of the Other Bumiputeras are the indigenous groups residing in the rural areas of Sabah and Sarawak.

The comparatively low proportion who have never attended school has naturally resulted in a lower proportion with tertiary education among this ethnic group. The educational attainment viewed in terms of

TABLE 6.7

Percentage Distribution of Population Aged 6 and Over by Educational Attainment, Citizenship and Ethnic Group, 2000

Educational Attainment	Citizens						Non-Citizens
	Malays	Other Bumiputeras	Chinese	Indians	Others	Total	
Primary	33.1	34.8	30.1	31.6	37.5	32.4	35.1
Secondary	43.2	37.1	46.8	49.6	36.1	46.6	25.6
Tertiary	11.0	4.6	12.1	9.1	6.7	10.4	5.2
Never Attended School	5.4	21.0	7.3	6.7	14.1	8.4	26.3
Unknown	1.3	2.5	3.7	2.9	5.6	2.2	7.8
Total	100.0	100.0	100.0	100.0	100.0	100.0	100.0

the three broad categories does not exhibit any marked differences among the Malays, Chinese and Indians. The tremendous progress made by the Malays is of course due to the admission policy of according special preferences to the Bumiputeras in particularly institutions of higher learning funded by the government. The Indians and particularly the Chinese enrol in private universities and in overseas universities.

CITIZENSHIP PATTERN

The granting of citizenship with all its attendant privileges and benefits has been jealously safeguarded in Malaysia with the enforcement of strict rules and procedures. According to the Federal Constitution, citizenship may be granted in one of the three ways, by operation of law, by registration or by naturalisation. The extent to which the population has assumed a more settled character can be examined in terms of the information on citizenship collected in population censuses. The item on citizenship was not included in the censuses conducted in Malaysia until the post-independence era after 1963 when the great concern for citizenship issues and political enfranchisement became part of the process of nation-building. However, the procedure employed to collect the information and the presentation of statistics in respect of citizenship have not been uniform in the post-Malaysia censuses.

In the first two censuses held in 1970 and 1980, the item on citizenship was used to collect information from respondents aged 12 and over. This particular cut-off point was linked to the issue of identity cards to all residents who are 12 years and older. A change was introduced in the last two censuses where the collection of citizenship information was applied to all respondents regardless of age.

The item on citizenship has assumed greater significance in recent years not only because proof of citizenship is necessary for voting and other purposes, but in the recent censuses reports many items of information have been presented in terms of the citizen population only and not the total population. A good example is the availability of statistics regarding ethnicity for the citizen population but not for the non-citizen population. We are therefore forced to study the affected statistics such as ethnicity and other characteristics in terms of the citizen population only. For sure, it would be more desirable and meaningful to look at certain characteristics of the population from the viewpoint of the overall population.

The first pan-Malaysia Census conducted in 1970 shows that out of a total population of 6,561,300 aged 12 years and over, some 6,074,834 or 92.6 per cent were enumerated as Malaysian citizens.[7] The position improved somewhat by the time of next census held in 1980 when 7,204,891 or 97.8 per cent aged 12 years and over were counted as Malaysian citizens.[8] Similar figures for the total population of all ages are not available, and hence comparison with the next two censuses cannot be made. The 12-year lower age limit as mentioned earlier, was linked to the compulsory registration for an identity card when one reaches the age of 12.

In 1991 the number of Malaysian citizens among the total population amounted to 16,812,300 or 95.7 per cent as compared with 21,889,900 or 94.1 per cent in 2000. During this intercensal period, the citizen population registered an increase of 30.2 per cent. This is in sharp contrast to the non-citizen population which grew by 84.4 per cent during the same period, boosting the figure from 751,100 to 1,384,800. This differential rate of increase continued during the postcensal years 2000–2005 when the citizen population rose by 27.5 per cent as against the 11.3 per cent recorded by the citizen population. The heavy inflow of migrant labour from particularly Indonesia and the Philippines in recent years has been responsible for the spectacular growth of the non-citizen population. Natural increase, the excess of births over deaths, has never played an important role in population growth among the non-citizens. In fact, many categories of female workers admitted to work in low-skilled jobs such as domestic maids are prohibited from producing babies, and will be repatriated on discovery of their pregnant status.

The regional distribution of the two groups of population, citizens and non-citizens, is laid out in Table 6.8. The first thing to note is that the distribution of the citizen population, as to be expected, is fairly similar to that of the total population, already discussed in an earlier chapter dealing Population Growth and Distribution. We will therefore confine our discussion to the non-citizen group. Out of the total of 1,765,700 non-citizens in 2000, a huge number, 746,500 or 42.3 per cent, were enumerated in Sabah. An extremely poor second was recorded by Selangor with 248,800 or 14.1 per cent, followed closely in third place occupied by Johore with 198,200 or 11.2 per cent. The Federal Territory of Kuala Lumpur had a fair number of non-citizens, 116,700 or 6.6 per cent. In all the other states, the non-citizens had a negligible presence.

TABLE 6.8
Distribution of Population by Citizenship and State, 2000

State	Number ('000)			Percentage		
	Citizen	Non-Citizen	Total	Citizen	Non-Citizen	Total
Johore	2,903.0	198.2	3,101.2	11.9	11.2	11.9
Kedah	1,807.1	41.0	1,848.1	7.4	2.3	7.1
Kelantan	1,476.1	29.5	1,505.6	6.1	1.7	5.8
Malacca	682.2	30.8	713.0	2.8	1.7	2.7
Negri Sembilan	907.1	39.2	946.3	3.7	2.2	3.6
Pahang	1,356.0	71.0	1,427.0	5.6	4.0	5.5
Penang	1,390.6	78.2	1,468.8	5.7	4.4	5.6
Perak	2,200.0	56.4	2,256.4	9.0	3.2	8.6
Perlis	220.4	4.1	224.5	0.9	0.2	0.9
Sabah	2,268.7	746.5	3,015.2	9.3	42.3	11.2
Sarawak	2,229.7	82.9	2,312.6	9.2	4.7	8.9
Selangor	4,487.3	248.8	4,736.1	18.4	14.1	18.1
Trengganu	994.2	22.3	1016.5	4.1	1.3	3.9
Kuala Lumpur	1,439.8	116.7	1,556.2	5.9	6.6	6.7
Total	24,362.0	1,765.7	26,127.7	100.0	100.0	100.0

The data given in Table 6.8 can also be analysed in terms of the two components of citizenship within the total population in each state. The most unique feature was displayed by Sabah where the proportion of non-citizens reached 23.5 per cent in 2000, with the citizens taking up to only 76.5 per cent. In the other states and Kuala Lumpur, the proportion of population enumerated as citizens stayed well above the level of 90 per cent. By and large, a higher proportion of citizens has continued to persist in the northern and eastern parts of West Malaysia, reaching 98.5 per cent in Perlis, 98.4 per cent in Kedah and Kelantan, and 98.2 per cent in Trengganu. Apart from the geographical remoteness of these states from the main stream of migration from particularly Indonesia, there are fewer employment opportunities for migrant workers in these states where economic activity and progress lacked behind the western states. A higher proportion of citizens was recorded in Kuala Lumpur with 93.3 per cent, Johore 94.5 per cent, and Selangor 95.6 per cent.

The impact of recent inflow of migrant workers is also visible in the composition of non-citizens according to their country of origin. Judging from our earlier comments in previous chapters, we should not be

TABLE 6.9
Distribution of Non-Citizen Population by Country of Origin and Sex, 2000

Country	Number			Percentage		
	Male	Female	Total	Male	Female	Total
Indonesia	392,036	322,844	714,880	57.2	59.6	58.3
Philippines	98,351	102,322	200,673	14.3	18.9	16.4
Bangladesh	63,551	1,489	65,040	9.3	0.3	5.3
Thailand	12,906	20,902	33,808	1.9	3.9	2.8
South Asia	17,824	10,724	28,548	2.6	2.0	2.3
Singapore	7,607	9,256	16,863	1.1	1.7	1.4
China	7,906	8,707	16,613	1.2	1.6	1.4
Japan	4,575	3,289	7,864	0.7	0.6	0.6
Pakistan	7,129	720	7,849	1.0	0.1	0.6
Myanmar	5,460	2,113	7,573	0.8	0.4	0.6
Others	16,839	14,037	30,876	2.5	2.6	2.5
Unknown	51,295	44,856	96,151	7.5	8.8	7.8
Total	685,479	541,259	1,226,738	100.0	100.0	100.0

surprised about the pre-eminence of Indonesia from which the non-citizens originated. The proportion reached 58.3 per cent, way ahead of the 16.4 per cent for the Philippines and 5.3 per cent for Bangladesh. Among the 714,880 non-citizens from Indonesia, they were mainly residing in Sabah (42.8 per cent), Selangor (15.0 per cent) and Johore (12.1 per cent). As for the 200,673 non-citizens from the Philippines, nearly all (96.6 per cent) were staying in Sabah. A greater spread was displayed by the 65,090 non-citizens from Bangladesh, 34.8 per cent in Selangor, 16.3 per cent in Johore, 13.9 per cent in Penang, and 8.3 per cent in Perak.

Notes

1. Saw Swee-Hock, *The Population of Peninsular Malaysia* (Singapore: Singapore University Press, 1988).
2. Malaysia, *Social Statistics Bulletin Malaysia* (Kuala Lumpur: Department of Statistics, 2005).
3. Malaysia, *Monthly Statistical Bulletin* (Kuala Lumpur: Department of Statistics, 2006).
4. Saw Swee-Hock, "The Dynamics of Ageing in Singapore", *Annals of the Academy of Medicine* 7, no. 2 (September 1985).
5. Shaari bin Abdul Rahman, *2000 Population and Housing Census, Education and Social Characteristics of the Population* (Kuala Lumpur: Department of Statistics, 2002).
6. Lee Hock Guan, "Globalisation and Ethnic Integration in Malaysian Education", in *Malaysia: Recent Trends and Challenge*, edited by Saw Swee-Hock and K. Kesavapany (Singapore: Institute of Southeast Asian Studies, 2005).
7. R. Chander, *1970 General Report: Population Census of Malaysia*, Volume 1 (Kuala Lumpur: Department of Statistics, 1977).
8. Khoo Teik Huat, *1980 General Report of the Population Census*, Volume 1 (Kuala Lumpur: Department of Statistics, 1983).

7

Nuptiality Trends and Patterns

In recent years nuptiality has come to be recognised as an integral part of the study of the demography of any country, largely because the formation and dissolution of marital unions have an important bearing on the level of fertility. We may regard marriage as an event that marks the beginning of the potential period of childbearing and marital dissolution as the end of this period. It is also recognised that age at marriage can affect the level of fertility and hence the rate of population growth. In this chapter an attempt is made to examine nuptiality trends and patterns in Malaysia during the postwar period.

Our study of nuptiality will be based on marital status data collected in the population censuses and classified into single, married, widowed and divorced. The data reflect unions in which the partners have participated in some form of legal marriage solemnised according to the various marriage laws. We should always bear in mind that the modern form of consensus unions among persons who have never been married according to either legal or customary rites is rather rare in Malaysia. We should also note that it is not possible to investigate nuptiality by means of comprehensive data derived from marriage registration records since such annual statistics have never been compiled and published regularly.

MARRIAGE CUSTOMS AND LAWS

The great diversity of religions that we have observed in an earlier chapter necessarily implies that it would be quite difficult to have a common legislation to govern all the various types of marriages taking place in the country. It was inevitable that over the years separate laws were introduced to regulate these marriages, which are solemnised according to the various religious and customary rites. There are one set of laws governing the marriage of persons both of whom are Muslim and another group of laws meant to regulate all the other marriages contracted between non-Muslims. Almost all these marriage laws have their roots during the colonial period, introduced in different parts of the country at different times as determined by the extent or concern of British rule or influence at that time.

The most important marriages are those contracted by persons both of whom profess the Islamic faith. Such Muslim marriages must be solemnised and registered under the provisions of the respective laws enacted by the state governments and the Federal Territory.[1] Examples of these regional laws are the Trengganu *Administration of Islamic Law Enactment*, 1955; Kedah *Administration of Muslim Law Enactment*, 1962; Perak *Administration of Muslim Law Enactment*, 1965; and *The Islamic Family Law (Federal Territory) Act*, 1984. If both parties are Muslims, they must marry according to the rules stipulated in the ordinances regardless of their racial origin. However, most of the Muslim marriages are contracted between Malays and a few are contracted between Indonesians, Pakistanis, Bangladeshis and Indians who follow the Islamic faith. The groom must be at least 18 years of age and the bride at least 16. In exceptional circumstances the Syariah judge may grant his permission to a man or woman below the minimum age to marry. By law Muslim marriages may be polygamous and the husband can take up to four wives at any point of time provided they are all treated equally. Most Muslim marriages are, however, monogamous.

Dissolution of Muslim marriages is governed by Islamic law which by tradition has allowed divorces to be affected in four different ways.[2] An easy and starkly simple method is for the husband to unilaterally divorce his wife by merely pronouncing *talak* three times in front of her at any time and place without the need for any witness to be present. If he pronounces one or two *talaks* only, the wife is also regarded as divorced but may not remarry another person for another 100 days. During this 100-day period known as *eddah*, the husband is allowed to change his mind and be reconciled with his wife. If the husband pronounces the three *talaks*, the divorce is irrevocable and the couple cannot be reunited as husband and wife unless she marries another man and is subsequently divorced. In some cases the husband, after rashly invoking three *talaks*, arranges for his ex-wife to marry another man on the understanding that he will quickly divorce her so that she may marry the first husband.

The second method is known as *fasakh* by which a divorce is granted to a wife by a religious judge in cases where the husband deserts and fails to maintain the wife or where the husband is impotent, or abjures Islam. The third method of divorce is known as *cerai taklik* which refers to the special conditions attached by the bride's guardian in the marriage contract. A divorce may be granted to the wife if it can be established that the husband has contravened these special conditions. Finally, a divorce by *khuluk* may be executed in cases where the wife seeks a divorce from a reluctant husband by offering him a sum of money or some form of property in compensation.

The other religious form of marriage refers to Christian marriages which were solemnised under the *Christian Marriage Ordinance, 1956*, Federation of Malaya, No. 33 of 1956, which was in operation in the 11 states of the West Malaysia from 1 August 1957 to 28 February 1982. Prior to the introduction of this act, Christian marriages were solemnised in the Straits Settlements under the *Christian Marriage Ordinance, 1898* and later the *Christian Marriage Ordinance, 1940*, in the Federated Malay States under the *Christian Marriage Enactment, 1915*, and in Johore, Kelantan and Kedah under similar enactments.[3] But there were no such enactment in Perlis and Trengganu allowing the solemnisation of Christian marriages prior to 1957.

Christian marriages may be contracted between Christians of all denominations. Such marriages may be contracted between Christians as well as between persons one of whom is a Christian. The minimum age for contracting Christian marriages is 21 for both the groom and bride, but grooms aged 16 to 20 and brides aged 14 to 20 can still marry with the written consent of the parents or guardians. Unlike Muslim marriages, Christian marriages are monogamous and take place among a wider range of ethnic groups. Christian marriages are solemnised by authorised person in churches or other religious institutions and are registered in the Registry of Marriages.

The third distinct type of marriage refers to those solemnised and registered according to the provisions of the *Civil Marriage Ordinance, 1952*, Federation of Malaya, No. 44 of 1952, which was in operation in the 11 states of West Malaysia from 1 January 1955 to 28 February 1982. The ordinance was intended to enable persons in the 11 states to contract, if they so desire, a monogamous civil marriage whatever might have been their religion, faith or custom.[4] Christians could choose to marry under the provisions of this ordinance, but Muslims were specifically prohibited from contracting civil marriages even if only one of the couple was a Muslim. Twenty-one was the minimum age required for both men and women to contract civil marriages but men aged 16 to 20 and women aged 14 to 20 may still contract marriages with the written consent of their parents. Prior to January 1955, civil marriages could only be contracted in the states of Penang and Malacca under the more restricted *Civil Marriage Ordinance, 1940*, Straits Settlements, No. 9 of 1940.

Apart from the above types of marriages governed by the three separate marriage laws, there were other marriages, which were contracted outside these laws according to religious or customary rites. Until February 1982 there were no laws compelling these miscellaneous marriages to be registered, but married couples could apply to the Registrar of Marriage for their marriages to be registered under the then *Registration of Marriage Ordinance, 1952*, Federation of Malaya, No. 53 of 1952, which came into force on 1 January 1955. Marriages could only be registered under this ordinance if neither one of the parties professed the Islamic or Christian religion and besides they must be effected within three months of the marriage date. Marriages registered under this ordinance could be polygamous if the Registrar was satisfied that the religion or custom governing these marriages permitted polygamy, and marriages not registered at all could be polygamous. What is important is that until February 1982 non-Muslim couples could choose to marry outside the ambit of any marriage laws, and could also decide not to have their marriages registered at all. This means that there is no complete registration of all marriages taking place in the country.

In an effort to accord greater rights and protection to non-Muslim women, the government streamlined the marriage laws by enacting the *Law Reform (Marriage and Divorce) Act, 1976*, Malaysia 1976, which came into force on 1 March 1982. This act was based on the recommendations of the Royal Commission on non-Muslim Marriage and Divorce Laws and was designed to eradicate the confusions, complications and injustices of the then domestic laws concerning the marriage and divorce of non-Muslims.[5] The act repeated all the previous laws, discussed earlier, governing non-Muslim marriages, but it does not affect the validity of marriages solemnised under any law, religion or custom prior to the appointed date of the act. The most outstanding feature of the act is that it abolishes polygamy among non-Muslims whose marriages were contracted from 1 March 1982.[6] Also it became compulsory for all non-Muslim marriages to be registered regardless of whether they were solemnised by the Registrar of Marriage in the Registry or by an authorised person in an approved place. The significance of this new act from the statistical point of view is that, coupled with the compulsory registration of Muslim marriages, there is complete registration of all marriages that occurred in the country from 1 March 1982. However, statistics of marriages solemnised under this act have yet to be compiled and published on a comprehensive and regular basis. Our analysis of nuptiality trends and patterns must by necessity depend on the marital status data published in the population census reports.

AGE AT FIRST MARRIAGE

An analysis of the average age at first marriage of women and men can be considered as a central piece in the study of nuptiality trends and patterns in any country. The age at marriage marks the beginning of marital formation on a permanent basis for the majority of the population, even though some may end up in divorce or separation. The age at marriage of women is recognised as one of the important factors that determine the level of fertility and hence the rate of population growth. The experience of many developing countries has demonstrated that the very low age at marriage of women has been the major factor responsible for the high level of fertility, particularly in situations where contraceptive use is negligible. A shift upward in this low marriage age is usually followed by a decline in fertility. In fact, the raising of the minimum marriage age for women through legislation has been resorted to by some developing countries as part of their overall strategy in trying to bring down the level of fertility.

Since the registration of marriages has been incomplete up to February 1982 and statistics based on complete registration after this date have yet to be compiled and published, it is not possible to calculate the average age at first marriage on an annual basis from registration records. Instead, we will study age at marriage in terms of the singulate mean age at marriage calculated from the population census years.[7] This method determines the mean age at first marriage for males and females in a synthetic censal cohort who marry for the first time before the age 50. The estimation of the mean age at marriage consists in finding the total number of years lived in the single state by a generation from birth to age 50 years, and dividing this total by the number who have been removed by marriage from the cohort. This gives the mean duration of single life which is equivalent to the average age at first marriage and described as the singulate mean age at marriage (SMAM). If s_x denotes the proportion single in the age group x to $x + 5$ and s the average

$$(s_{45} + s_{50}) \div 2, \text{ then SMAM} = \frac{\left(5 \times \sum_{x=0}^{45} s_x - 50_s\right)}{1 - s}$$

According to the above formula, the singulate mean age at marriage for the men and women for the three latest censuses was computed and the results are presented in Table 7.1. It is customary to look at the average age at marriage for the two sexes separately in view of the unique factors determining the marriage age of each sex. It would not be meaningful to examine the marriage age for both sexes combined. The singulate mean age at marriage for women rose from 23.5 years in 1980 to 24.7 years in 1991, giving a rise of 1.2 years or 5.1 per cent. In latest intercensal period, the advance in average marriage age was slowed down to a rise of only 0.4 years of 1.6 per cent.

TABLE 7.1
Singulate Mean Age at First Marriage by
Sex and Urban/Rural Area, 1980–2000

Year	Male	Female	Age Gap
		Total	
1980	26.6	23.5	3.1
1991	28.2	24.7	3.5
2000	28.6	25.1	3.5
		Urban	
1980	27.5	24.8	2.7
1991	28.4	25.4	3.0
2000	28.9	25.7	3.2
		Rural	
1980	26.0	22.6	3.4
1991	27.9	23.7	4.2
2000	28.1	23.8	4.3

The continuous uptrend in the singulate mean age at marriage of women may be attributed to a combination of factors. Among the more important ones were the normalisation of the sex ratio of marriageable ages, the enhanced educational attainment of women, the greater female participation in the modern sectors of the economy, and the changing attitude towards marriage as influenced by modenisation. The uptrend in the marriage age of women was also experienced in many developing countries where fundamental social and economic changes have been taking place.[8] The rise in the marriage age of women has been one of the major factors influencing fertility decline in many countries.

The men, by comparison, experienced a faster advance in their average age at marriage during the first intercensal period, rising by 1.6 years or 6.0 per cent to bring the figure to 28.2 years in 1991 from 26.6 years in 1980. This may perhaps be due to the uneven sex ratio with more men than women. The surplus of male mates engendered the marriage squeeze whereby the men were forced to marry at an older age.[9] What it means is that as the sex ratio moved towards a more balanced position in recent years, the availability of prospective female mates improved and men need not continue to marry at older ages. The singulate mean age at marriage rose from 28.2 years in 1991 to 28.6 in 2000, an increase of only 0.4 years or 1.4 per cent. The diverse movement in the marriage age between the two sexes obviously has an impact on the gap in marriage age. The age gap stood at 3.1 years in 1980, and rose to 3.5 years in 1991 and remained so in 2000.

It is known that the average age at first marriage varies between the urban and rural areas, with the town folk marrying at an older age than the rural inhabitants.[10] This aspect of the marriage can be analysed in Malaysia. From the census data on marital status tabulated according to urban/rural classification, one can compute the single mean age at marriage for each of these two areas, the results are presented in Table 7.1. It may be observed that the average marriage age of men in 1980 was 27.5 years in the urban area, about 1.5 years higher than the average of 26.0 in the rural area. In the case of the women, the two figures were 24.8 years in the urban area and 22.6 years in the rural area, giving a bigger differential of 2.2 years. This larger differential experienced by the women persisted into 1991 and 2000.

The other highlight underlined by the figures given in Table 7.1 refers to the wider gap between the male and female marriages age in the rural than in the urban area. In the latter, the average marriage age was 27.5 years for men and 24.8 years for women in 1980, giving a gap of 2.7 years. In the rural area, the two corresponding figures were 26.0 years and 22.6 years, resulting in a bigger age gap of 3.4 years. This pattern continued to prevail in 1991 and 2000. Greater significance should be attached to the differential in female marriage age in view of its impact on the differences in the level of fertility between the urban and rural areas.

The statistics required to calculate the singulate mean age at marriage for the ethnic groups are also made available in the population censuses. However, it may be recalled that the ethnic classification is only made available for the Malaysian citizen component of the total population in the 1991 and 2000 Censuses.[11] We should therefore bear in mind that the singulate mean age at marriage for the main ethnic groups given in Table 7.2 refer to those who were citizens only. The average marriage age for the total citizen population was computed as 27.8 years for the male citizens and 24.8 years for the female citizens in 1991. Both these figures for the non-citizen population were lower, 26.8 years for men and 21.4 years for women. The significantly lower marriage age for the non-citizen population was clearly due to the foreign women originating from the neighbouring countries where the women tend to marry at a very early age.

Similar data for the main ethnic groups are available for the citizen population only in the last two censuses and for the total population in

TABLE 7.2

Singulate Mean Age at First Marriage by
Sex, Ethnic Group and Citizenship, 1991–2000

Ethnic Group	1991			2000		
	Male	Female	Age Group	Male	Female	Age Group
CITZENS	27.8	24.8	3.0	28.6	25.1	3.5
Malays	27.5	24.6	2.9	27.9	24.8	3.1
Other Bumiputeras	25.5	22.1	3.4	26.9	23.1	3.8
Chinese	29.8	26.3	3.5	30.6	27.0	3.6
Indians	28.3	25.5	2.8	28.8	25.4	3.4
Others	27.9	24.0	3.9	28.3	24.4	3.9
NON-CITIZENS	26.8	21.4	5.4	28.7	24.4	4.3

the censuses held in 1980 and earlier.[12] There is therefore a break in comparative data, and hence only the figures for 1991 and 2000 are provided in Table 7.2. It may be observed that these figures bring out not only some similarities but also interesting differences among the ethnic groups with respect to their average age at first marriage. Among the women in 1991, the highest average marriage age was experienced by the Chinese women (26.3 years), the second highest by the Indians (25.5 years), the third by the Malays (24.6 years), and the lowest by the Other Bumiputeras (22.1 years). The last ethnic group comprised of mainly the diverse indigenous women who usually marry at a young age. The pattern of average marriage age among these ethnic groups was maintained nine years later in 2000.

Interestingly, the above relative position of the singulate mean age at marriage was also experienced by the men of these ethnic groups in 1991, and remained to be so in 2000. The consistency in the relative position of average marriage age across ethnic groups and census dates is a reflection of the tenacious influence of the factors determining the age at which men and women first marry. Without any exception, the universal feature of higher average marriage age for men than for women was also noticeable among the ethnic groups in the two census years.

MARITAL STATUS COMPOSITION

In our study of marital status, we will use the data on persons aged 15 and over, though the censuses collected this information from young respondents below age 15. In the tabulation at age, it was ascertained that there was only a handful of these young persons who have ever married. It is customary to classify marital status into four categories, viz. single or never married, married, widowed and divorced, at the time of enumeration. Single is defined to include persons who have never married. Married refers to persons who were currently married at the time of enumeration, and they would include those married by law or by religious rites or were living together by mutual agreement. Widowed refers to those whose marriages have been terminated through death of their spouses and have not remarried. Divorced refers to persons whose marriages have been terminated through divorce by law or religious arrangement or separated for a long duration without any possibility of reconciliation.

TABLE 7.3

Distribution of Population Aged 15 and Over by Marital Status and Sex, 1980–2000

Marital Status	Male			Female		
	1980	1991	2000	1980	1991	2000
	Number ('000)					
Single	1,541.1	2,166.0	3,107.2	1,217.7	1,661.8	2,397.3
Married	2,236.0	3,238.2	4,596.8	2,326.3	3,335.1	4,618.4
Widowed	81.9	94.9	128.9	367.6	453.0	549.6
Divorced	26.7	26.5	31.5	83.9	85.7	93.9
Total	3,885.5	5,525.6	7,884.4	3,995.6	5,535.6	7,659.2
	Percentage					
Single	39.7	39.2	39.0	30.5	30.0	30.9
Married	57.5	58.6	58.9	58.2	60.2	60.6
Widowed	2.1	1.7	1.7	9.2	8.2	7.2
Divorced	0.7	0.5	0.4	2.1	1.5	1.2
Total	100.0	100.0	100.0	100.0	100.0	100.0

The distribution of the population age of 15 and over according to the above four-fold classification is presented in Table 7.3. Consequent on the growth of the population aged 15 and over, every one category of the marital status naturally recorded an increase during the whole period from 1980 to 2000. A somewhat more interesting picture is revealed by a comparison of the male and female figures at any of the three census years. The number of divorced women has always been about three times that of divorced men because less divorced women tend to remarry. Again, widows exceeded widowers by slightly more than four times and this is due to the longer life expectancy of women. The difference among the married category was by comparison, very negligible, with slightly more married women than men. A completely opposite picture was underlined by the figures for the single category; there were conspicuously more single men than women.

PROPORTION SINGLE

The next aspect of nuptiality that we will examine is the proportion of the population remaining single, an important index measuring the extent of marriage formation and childbearing. The proportion single is influenced, among others, by the average age at marriage discussed earlier. Table 7.4 presents the figures for the percentage of the population aged 15 and over who had remained single at the time of the census for the citizen and non-citizen population separately. Also included are the figures for the main ethnic groups within the citizen population. The exclusion of young persons below age 15 would have virtually no impact on our analysis since almost everyone in this group would be single.

There is a clear difference in the proportion single prevailing among the citizen and non-citizen population. In 1991 the proportion of male citizens remaining single was 38.9 per cent as against the high of 43.9 per cent for the male non-citizens. This notable differential has remained unchanged in 2000. The single male foreign workers among the non-citizens have less restrictions at home to impede them moving into Malaysia to work. This is not so in the case of the female foreign workers as manifested in the proportion of single among the non-citizens being only slightly higher than that among the citizens. The two respective proportions were 30.0 per cent and 30.4 per cent in 1999 and also 32.0 per cent and 30.9 per cent in 2000.

Before commenting on the proportion single among the main ethnic groups within the citizen population, the stable local component subjected to more traditional influences affecting nuptiality, we will discuss the factors affecting the proportion single. In the early days there was a decidedly strong belief that the prime function of women is to marry and

TABLE 7.4

Proportion of Single Persons Aged 15 and Over by Sex, Ethnic Group and Citizenship, 1991 and 2000

Ethnic Group	Male		Female	
	1991	2000	1991	2000
CITIZENS	38.9	38.6	30.4	30.9
Malays	38.3	38.3	30.4	30.9
Other Bumiputeras	36.4	37.5	25.5	28.0
Chinese	40.6	39.5	31.8	31.7
Indians	39.7	38.8	32.1	31.3
Others	37.4	40.3	28.1	32.8
NON-CITIZENS	43.9	43.8	30.9	32.0

raise a family, and spinsterhood finds little social acceptance among the public at large. But changing attitudes towards spinsterhood, improved education of women, and greater and more meaningful job opportunities for women inevitably lead to more women remaining single. The proportion single among the total female population aged 15 and over rose from 26.1 per cent in 1970 to 30.5 per cent in 1980,[13] while the proportion among the citizen female population rose from 30.4 per cent in 1991 to 30.9 per cent in 2000.

For the reasons cited above, the proportion single among female Other Bumiputeras was raised from 25.5 per cent in 1991 to 28.0 per cent. The Malay women, on the other hand, saw only a small rise in their proportion single from 30.4 per cent to 30.9 per cent during the same nine-year period. There was even a fall in the proportion single among the Chinese women, from 31.8 per cent to 31.7 per cent, and among the Indian women, from 32.1 per cent to 31.3 per cent during the same period. It would appear that the level of proportion single among these women from the main ethnic groups has stabilised and will be subjected to only very minor changes in the years ahead. In fact, the proportion single experienced by the Malay men had remained the same at 38.3 per cent, and the men of the other ethnic groups have undergone only minor changes.

A universal feature of nuptiality that is also noticeable in Table 7.4 refers to the greater tendency among men to remain single. This characteristic may be seen to exist at the two censuses and among all ethnic groups. But there was the decisive development towards a narrowing of the difference in the proportion single between the two sexes. This difference was narrowed from 7.9 to 7.4 percentage points for the Malays, from 10.9 to 9.5 percentage points for the Other Bumiputeras from 8.8 to 7.8 percentage points. This narrowing of the difference was brought about by a relatively greater rise in the female proportion, a reflection of the greater equality accorded to women in every sphere of their life in particularly education and employment.

For a better appreciation of the changes in the proportion single, we will move on to examine the percentages of single persons in the various quinary age group. In Table 7.5 are given the figures for the age-specific proportion single by sex for the three latest censuses. A distinctive pattern of variation with age is disclosed by these figures. For the men, the proportion single commences just below 100 per cent in the youngest age group 15–19, and falls rapidly until the mid-thirties and then very

TABLE 7.5
Proportion of Single Persons by Sex and Age Group, 1980–2000

Age Group	Male			Female		
	1980	1991	2000	1980	1991	2000
15–19	98.7	98.6	98.9	89.7	92.4	95.1
20–24	80.4	85.7	88.2	51.3	60.2	68.5
25–29	39.9	49.0	54.8	20.9	25.9	29.7
30–34	14.5	20.4	24.7	9.9	12.4	12.7
35–39	7.2	10.0	12.3	5.3	7.8	7.8
40–44	4.9	6.0	7.4	3.7	5.7	6.1
45–49	4.0	4.0	5.1	3.0	3.8	5.0
50–54	3.4	3.2	3.8	2.2	2.7	4.1
55–59	3.0	2.6	2.9	1.7	2.3	2.9
60–64	3.0	2.3	2.3	1.9	1.7	2.3
65 & Over	3.8	1.9	2.1	2.1	1.4	1.7

gently until the old age groups where only about 3 per cent still remains single. By and large, the women exhibit the same shape, but the curve is always lower than that of the males throughout the whole age range.

The variations in the proportion remaining single in 2000 in the states of West Malaysia for each of the two sexes are portrayed in Table 7.6. Without any exception, the proportion of single persons aged 15 and over, was higher for the men than the women in all the states. The more important feature concerns the fairly strong tendency for the urbanised and industrialised states to have a higher proportion of single persons than the predominantly rural agricultural states. Good examples are the relatively higher proportion of spinsters in Kuala Lumpur (37.8 per cent), Selangor (34.4 per cent) and Penang (33.9 per cent) and the lower proportion in Perlis (25.5 per cent), Kelantan (26.9 per cent) and Kedah (27.8 per cent). Moving on to the male figures, we can observe the same regional pattern in the proportion of men remaining single. This pattern existing among both the sexes is a reflection of the fact that people residing in the less developed areas tend to marry earlier than their counterparts living in the more developed areas where the modernisation influence leading to later marriages is more pervasive.

TABLE 7.6
Proportion of Single Persons Aged 15 and Over by Sex and State, 2000

State	Male	Female
Johore	40.7	30.8
Kedah	35.0	27.8
Kelantan	34.0	26.9
Malacca	38.8	31.1
Negri Sembilan	39.8	29.7
Pahang	37.7	28.2
Penang	39.9	33.9
Perak	36.8	28.0
Perlis	31.3	25.5
Sabah	38.6	30.4
Sarawak	36.0	28.3
Selangor	41.3	34.4
Trengganu	39.7	30.1
Kuala Lumpur	43.7	37.8

PROPORTION DIVORCED

Among those who do not remain single, their marriage may be dissolved through death of one spouse leading to widowhood or incompatibility leading to divorce or separation. Widowhood, being nothing more than a function of mortality level, conforms to a predictable pattern, while the incidence of divorce is determined by a variety of factors, including the laxity or otherwise of the laws concerning marital dissolution. Non-Muslim divorces are effected in accordance to the *Law Reform (Marriage and Divorce) Act 1976* mentioned earlier, while Muslim divorces are conducted according to Islamic law. As mentioned earlier, the dissolution of Muslim marriages is governed by the law of Islam, which had traditionally permitted divorce to be effected in four different ways.[14] They are known as *talaks, fasakh, cerai taklik* and *khuluk*.

In Table 7.7 are provided the figures for the proportion of divorced persons aged 15 and over by sex, citizenship and ethnic group for the last two censuses. It should be emphasised that these figures refer to persons who have been formally divorced by law as well as those who have permanently separated from their spouses. A common feature of the

TABLE 7.7

**Proportion of Divorced Persons Aged 15 and Over
by Sex, Ethnic Group and Citizenship, 1991 and 2000**

Ethnic Group	Male		Female	
	1991	2000	1991	2000
CITIZENS	0.5	0.4	1.5	1.2
Malays	0.5	0.4	2.0	1.5
Other Bumiputeras	0.7	0.6	2.2	1.6
Chinese	0.3	0.4	0.7	0.7
Indians	0.4	0.3	0.9	0.9
Others	0.6	0.7	1.7	1.4
NON-CITIZENS	0.9	0.5	2.6	1.8

table is the lower proportion of divorced persons among men than among women. This is in part due to the generally greater social stigma attached to female divorces and hence their chances of re-marrying are less than that of the divorced men. The other interesting feature refers to the much higher proportion of divorced women among the Malays and the Other Bumiputeras, undoubtedly caused by the relatively easy Islamic laws whereby divorces are permitted. For example, the proportion divorced in 2000 was 1.5 per cent for the Malay women and 1.6 per cent for the Other Bumiputera women as compared to the low of 0.7 per cent for the Chinese women and 0.9 per cent for the Indian women.

The higher incidence of divorce among the Bumiputera community will be the key factor in determining the variation in the proportion of divorced persons in different parts of the country. The proportion divorced was directly linked to ethnic composition; states with a bigger proportion of Bumiputera population will have a higher proportion of divorced persons. This is clearly revealed by the female figures in Table 7.8 where the relatively high proportion of divorced women was recorded in Kelantan (2.6 per cent), Trengganu (2.1 per cent) and Perlis (1.9 per cent). The lowest proportion of divorced women was recorded in the two western states of Selangor and Johore, both with 0.9 per cent.

Apart from the above population census data, there are some divorce statistics that can be derived from the marriage registration office. Shirle Gordon and Judith Djamour have compiled some Muslim marriage and divorce statistics on a state basis.[15] According to these statistics, there

TABLE 7.8

Proportion of Divorced Persons Aged 15 and Over by Sex and State, 2000

State	Male	Female
Johore	0.3	0.9
Kedah	0.5	1.5
Kelantan	0.7	2.6
Malacca	0.3	1.2
Negri Sembilan	0.3	1.1
Pahang	0.3	1.0
Penang	0.4	1.0
Perak	0.4	1.0
Perlis	0.6	1.9
Sabah	0.6	1.4
Sarawak	0.5	1.3
Selangor	0.3	0.9
Trengganu	0.5	2.1
Kuala Lumpur	0.4	1.4

were 116,767 Muslim marriages and 90,296 Muslim divorces registered during 1948–1957 in Kelantan, giving a divorce rate of 77.3 per cent. For the same period in Trengganu, there were 54,791 Muslim marriages and 39,052 Muslim divorces, a rate of 71.3 per cent. The three corresponding figures for Perlis were 9,382, 6,678 and 71.2 per cent.

The frequent marital dissolution among the Muslim section of the Bumiputera population may be attributed to a variety of causes. First and foremost, we have already observed earlier the relative case with which a husband can divorce his wife under Islamic law, and the *syariah* court might not be very strict with couples seeking divorce nor did it provide adequate conciliatory services. The second reason is that there is an absence of any strong social sanctions against marital dissolution, and a divorced woman carries little stigma, and certainly more so in the case of a man. Divorce is culturally accepted and remarriage of divorced persons is expected and sanctioned. Another possible reason is that the economic deterrents are not very strong. A divorced woman with custody of children could always depend on her close kin for financial support, her children could be taken care of by her relatives, and remarriage would be possible and not be an expensive affair.

Notes

1. Ahmad bin Mohamad Ibrahim, "Developments in Marriage Laws in Malaysia and Singapore", *Malaya Law Review* 2, no. 2, December 1970.
2. See, for instance, M.B. Hooker, *Islamic Law in South-East Asia* (Oxford University Press, 1984) and Mohamed Din Bin Ali, "Malay Customary Law and Family", *Intisari* 2, no. 2, 1965.
3. Federation of Malaya, *Report of the Registrar-General on Population, Births, Deaths, Marriages and Adoptions, 1956* (Kuala Lumpur: Government Press, 1956).
4. Federation of Malaya, *Report of the Registrar-General on Population, Births, Deaths, Marriages and Adoptions, 1955* (Kuala Lumpur: Government Press, 1956).
5. *The Malay Mail*, 10 March 1970.
6. For a detailed discussion of this piece of new legislation, see Rafiah Salam, "The Legal Status of Women in a Multi-Racial Malaysian Society" in Hing Ai Yun et al. (eds.), *Women in Malaysia* (Kuala Lumpur: Pelanduk Publications, 1984).
7. John Hajnal, "Age at Marriage and Proportion Marrying", *Population Studies* 7, no. 2, November 1953.
8. See, for example, Peter C. Smith, "Asian Marriage Patterns in Transition", *Journal of Family History* 5, no. 1 (1980).
9. Ruth B. Dixon, "Explaining Cross-Cultural Variations in age at Marriage and Proportion Never Marrying", *Population Studies* 25, no. 1 (July 1971).
10. Saw Swee-Hock, *The Population of Peninsular Malaysia* (Singapore: Singapore University Press, 1988).
11. Haji Aziz bin Othman, *2000 General Report of the Population and Housing Census* (Kuala Lumpur: Department of Statistics, 2005).
12. Ibid.
13. Khoo Teik Huat, *1980 General Report of the Population Census* (Kuala Lumpur: Department of Statistics, 1983).
14. M.B. Hooker, *Islamic Law in Southeast Asia* (Kuala Lumpur: Oxford University Press, 1984) and Mohamed Din bin Ali, "Malay Customary Law and Family", *Intisari* 2, no. 2 (1965).
15. Shirle Gordon, "Malay Marriage/Divorce in the Eleven States of Malaya and Singapore", *Intisari* 2, no. 2 (n.d.) and Judith Djamour, *The Muslim Matrimonial Court in Singapore* (London: Athlone Press, 1966).

8

Fertility and Mortality

The size and structure of the population of Malaysia at any point of time are determined by the interactions of migration, fertility and mortality in the immediate past. While an earlier chapter has dealt with migration, this chapter will be devoted to an account of fertility and mortality. As in any country, the statistics required for the analysis of mortality and fertility are derived from the compulsory registration of births and deaths. The registration system is under the overall charge of the Registrar-General in the National Registration Department, and in each state there is a Registrar in charge of the Registration Department. In each state there are also registration centres situated in hospitals, police stations and city halls in urban centres, while in the rural areas registration of vital events can be made with authorised persons such as village headmen, headmasters and estate managers. The registration laws stipulate that the time allowed for registration is 14 days for live-births and still-births and 12 hours for deaths.

The birth and death statistics are compiled and published by the Department of Statistics. The vital statistics published by the Department of Statistics since the formation of Malaysia in 1963 are not comprehensive and uniform from year to year. For most years, the statistics are more comprehensive for West Malaysia than for East Malaysia, and hence the absence of national figures for the whole of Malaysia. Some of the difficulties encountered in obtaining national figures will be discussed in our analysis of the published data in regard to certain aspects of fertility and mortality discussed in this chapter.

POPULATION CONTROL PROGRAMME

The provision of family planning services on an organised basis dates back to 21 October 1954 when the Family Planning Association of

Selangor was officially established as a voluntary organisation.[1] With the support of individuals, firms and foundations, the Association was able to open two clinics in Kuala Lumpur in January 1954. These clinics, the first two of its kind in the country, ran only weekly sessions after office hours with the assistance of volunteers. In the early days the clinics were fairly well attended by many women and, encouraged by this modest success, more clinics were established in Selangor. Between July 1954 and August 1959 similar associations were formed in the states of Johore, Perak and Malacca, and family planning services were made available in clinics operated by these associations.

The need to establish a national organisation to coordinate and strengthen the family planning movement in the country became increasing evident in the mid-1950s. This aim was finally realised in May 1958 which saw the formation of the Federation of Family Planning Associations (FFPA), incorporating all the then existing state associations.[2] In the remaining states similar associations were set up between May 1961 and May 1962, and they automatically became members of the FFPA. The main source of finance for the FFPA is the annual grant from the International Planned Parenthood Federation (IPPF) and from the government. In 1981 the grant from the IPPF amounted to $842,000, while the government grant was $200,000. Many individuals and institutional well-wishers also contributed gifts in kind and cash.

The number of attendances at the various clinics operated by the state associations rose sharply over the years. For instance, the total number of attendances at all the clinics in the country increased from 19,654 in 1962 to 237,997 in 1967, the year when government family planning clinics were first introduced. Thereafter, attendances at FFPA clinics naturally suffered a small setback, and more so with progressively more services offered by the government. In 1981 the FFPA attendances totalled 223,250, and out of the total number of 56,869 patients who visited the clinics during the year, 10,324 were new acceptors and the remaining 46,545 were previous patients. Though there are no precise data, it would appear that the cumulative total of new acceptors since 1954 was in the order of 200,000.

The work of the private associations up to 1967 demonstrated that there was an increasing demand for family planning services among women of all educational groups in the country. In fact, the results of the first National Family Planning Survey conducted in 1967–67 confirmed that the associations could never have catered to the needs of all these women. It was estimated that some 201,700 women on the eve of the government programme in 1967 would like to practise birth control immediately or very soon.[3] Further, an additional 104,500 women were estimated to like to practise birth control after one or more births and 211,500 more after two or more births. In this respect the institution of a government programme in 1967 was quite timely.

The government adopted a positive population policy in its First Five-Year Plan 1966–70 which specifically advocated the introduction of a national population control programme to reduce the rate of population growth.[4] It was acknowledged that a reduction in the national birth rate was an important goal closely associated with the overall economic objective of raising aggregate as well as per capita income levels. The principal objective of the policy was the reduction of the then existing population growth of 3 per cent per annum to 2 per cent over a 20-year period. It was felt that if the rate of population increase remained at the existing level, the rate of growth of national income would be adversely affected in the years ahead because a large share of the increased income derived from economic growth would have to be diverted towards consumption in supporting a rapidly growing population rather than productive investment. In early 1966 the Malaysian Parliament passed the *Family Planning Act, 1966* under which the National Family Planning Board (NFPB) was established as an inter-ministerial organisation having statutory powers and a considerable degree of autonomy.[5]

The National Family Planning Board was formed on 10 June 1966 in an official ceremony with the inaugural address delivered by the Chairman of the Board and the government policy on birth control proclaimed by the Deputy Prime Minister.[6] At the same time plans were immediately made to launch a Family Planning Survey to collect baseline data to plan an action programme and to evaluate the work from time to time. The main objectives of the Board as spelt out in the Act are as follows:

(a) the formulation of policies and methods for the promotion and spread of family planning knowledge;
(b) the programming, directing, administering and coordinating of family planning activities;
(c) the training of all persons involved in the family planning extension work;

(d) the conducting of research on medical and biological methods related to family planning;

(e) the promotion of studies and research into inter-relationships between social, cultural, economic and population changes as well as research concerning fertility and maternity patterns;

(f) the setting up of a system of evaluation in order to assess the effectiveness of the programme and the progress towards the attainment of national objectives.

The Board was therefore conceived as part of an integrated movement to tackle the population problem but the population growth rate objective was given greater prominence in the early discussions of population policy.[7]

The members of the Board consists of a Chairman, a Director-General, 10 members representing government departments or ministries, and another 10 representing the non-government sector.[8] The Director-General serves as the Chief Executive of the NFPB. The day-to-day operation is shared among four major divisions, viz. Administration, Finance and Supply Division, Service and Training Division, Information, Education and Communication Division and Research, Evaluation and Management Information System Division. At the state level there is a State Officer in charge of family planning.

The national family planning programme was implemented in four main stages with Phase One in the metropolitan areas and extending gradually to the rural areas in Phase Four. Phase One was launched in May 1967 in the eight largest towns with a government maternity hospital each, and Phase Two was put into effect in the following year in the smaller towns with some 50 district hospitals. Phase Three was to cover the health centres and sub-centres in the rural areas, while Phase Four was meant to cover the other rural areas, which have no health centres at all but which could be reached through a combination of mobile clinics and *Kampong bidans*. The state clinics under the national programme were established in General Hospitals, District Hospitals, Maternity Hospitals, Main Health Centres, Health Sub-Centres and FELDA Midwife Clinic-cum-Quarters. Some difficulties due mainly to the lack of resources were encountered in the last two phases, and in the early 1970s some adjustments were introduced whereby family planning services were functionally integrated into the rural health services of the Ministry of Health as part of the total package for family planning for the populace. This Integration Programme was subsequently strengthened by the Population and Family Health Project.[9]

The Board commenced to offer family planning services in May 1967 in its clinics established in the large towns, and distributed mainly oral contraceptive pills and intra-uterine contraceptive devices (IUDs). During the first month 393 acceptors were recruited and by the end of the year the total number stood at 8,247. With the opening of more clinics, the number of acceptors rose sharply to 43,058 in 1968 and then to 48,140 in 1969. Since the Board also compiled statistics of acceptors recruited by the state Family Planning Association, estates, and government and private doctors, figures for the whole country were made available. The figures according to the main agencies are given in Table 8.1. The combined total number of acceptors recruited by all four agencies came to 20,726 in 1967. In 1968, the Board's first full year of clinic service, the grand total from all agencies was 74,935, and with saturation effect coming into play, the number dropped to the low of

TABLE 8.1
Family Planning Acceptors by Agency, 1967–1983

Year	NFPB	Integrated Programme	FPA	Others	Total
1967	8,247	—	10,132	2,347	20,726
1968	43,058	—	25,158	6,719	74,935
1969	48,140	—	16,695	5,740	70,575
1970	39,441	—	13,495	3,045	55,981
1971	36,159	2,962	13,205	2,441	54,767
1972	35,011	4,904	12,957	3,545	56,417
1973	35,458	4,627	12,059	5,168	57,312
1974	36,628	7,422	12,379	5,251	61,680
1975	37,673	14,809	11,839	5,027	69,348
1976	36,050	22,894	11,515	4,751	75,210
1977	36,472	25,222	10,619	8,063	80,376
1978	36,881	24,670	10,750	7,861	80,162
1979	34,509	32,246	14,070	6,435	87,260
1980	32,446	31,195	15,013	2,409	81,063
1981	30,137	28,010	13,717	2,864	74,728
1982	29,032	27,402	13,300	2,592	72,326
1983	25,580	25,696	11,929	1,856	65,061

54,767 in 1971. Thereafter, the number increased consistently to touch the peak of 87,260 in 1969, and then went down to reach 65,061 in 1983. As expected, some potential acceptors were diverted from other agencies to the Board's clinics. The more significant point is that without the Board's clinical services for a full year prior to 1968, there were only some 27,000 acceptors for the whole country but this figure increased by about threefold in 1969.

The overall targets of the national programme were clearly stated in the various Five-Year Development Plans. The First Malaysia Plan 1966–70 targeted for a reduction in the crude birth rate from 37.3 per 1,000 population in 1966 to 35.0 in 1970. This implied a recruitment of some 343,000 acceptors during the five-year period from both programme and non-programme sources. By the end of the period about 274,000 acceptors or 80 per cent of the target were successfully recruited. The crude birth rate, however, fell below the target to reach 32.6 in 1970. The Second Malaysia Plan 1971–75 called for a reduction in the crude birth rate from 35.0 to 30.0 and a recruitment of 535,000 acceptors from programme and non-programme sources.[10] At the end of the period the achievement was some 433,000 acceptors or 81 per cent, and the crude birth rate fell to 30.5 in 1975. Under the Third Malaysia Plan 1976–80, the crude birth rate was targeted to be lowered from 31.0 to 28.2 and the number of acceptors were fixed at 550,000. The actual figures turned out to be some 450,000 acceptors or 80 per cent and a birth rate of 30.3 in 1980. The Fourth Malaysia Plan 1981–85 calls for a reduction in the birth rate from 28.2 to 26.0 and a recruitment of 518,000 acceptors. The persistence of the birth rate above the targeted level in the last three plans is due to the increasing proportion of women in the reproductive ages to the total population.

Before the end of the Fourth Plan the government introduced a major shift in the national programme by adopting a new policy of achieving a population of 70 million by the year 2100. This target of 70 million was first mooted by the Prime Minister in his address to the United Malay National Organisation (UMNO) general assembly in September 1982 and officially announced by him in Parliament in April 1984 in his presentation of the mid-term review of the Fourth Plan. The new policy naturally led to a de-emphasis of family planning and a change in the name of NFPB to National Population and Family Development Board. The new policy, aimed at establishing a larger consumer base to generate and support industrial growth, does not affect the fertility trends and differentials up to 1983 that we will discuss in the following section. It will have an impact on the future course of fertility and hence the future trends in the population of the country, which will be dealt with in considerable detail in the last chapter.

FERTILITY TRENDS

In Table 8.2 we have presented the births and crude birth rates in terms of three-year periods since 1970 in order to remove the annual fluctuations and to enable us to concentrate on the long-term movements. The population denominator adopted in the calculation of the rates refers to the average of the three mid-year populations in each given period. The movement in the annual average number of births was generally upwards during the first two-and-a-half decades, increasing by 49.1 per cent from 362,469 in 1970–1972 to 540,417 in 1994–1996. Thereafter, a general downturn became apparent, with the number falling to 529,017 in 1997–1999, rising slightly to 532,104 in the next three-year period, and falling again in the final period 2003–2005.

A completely different path was followed by the crude birth rate during the same period. Commencing from 32.5 births per thousand

TABLE 8.2
Annual Average Births and Crude Birth Rates, 1970–2005

Period	Annual Average Births	Crude Birth Rate	Percentage Change	
			Births	Rate
1970–1972	362,469	32.5	—	—
1973–1975	372,428	31.0	+2.7	−4.6
1976–1978	390,751	30.3	+4.9	−2.3
1979–1981	420,078	30.8	+7.5	+1.7
1982–1984	462,138	30.7	+10.0	−0.3
1985–1987	496,913	38.4	+7.5	−1.0
1988–1990	496,615	28.1	−0.6	−7.6
1991–1993	527,296	28.1	+6.2	0.0
1994–1996	540,417	26.9	+2.5	−4.3
1997–1999	529,017	24.3	−2.1	−9.7
2000–2002	532,104	22.2	+0.6	−8.6
2003–2005	514,500	20.1	−3.3	−9.5

population, the rate continued to decline over the years, except during the period 1979–1981 when it rose by a mere 1.7 per cent. By the time of the latest period 2003–2005, the rate had been lowered by 3.8 per cent to reach 20.1. It is however important to emphasise that fertility has declined by this amount during the 35 years because the crude birth rate is not a good measure of the fertility level of a population. This is due to the fact that the rate is affected or distorted by the proportion of women in the reproductive ages of 15 to 45 to the total population. The best index for measuring fertility is the total fertility rate (TFR), which may be defined as the average number of children produced by a woman during her whole reproductive period.

The computation of the total fertility rate requires the birth statistics tabulated according to five-year age groups of mothers and the corresponding female population tabulated according to the similar five-year age groups. In the case of Malaysia, the second set of statistics pertaining to the female population is available, but the first set of statistics pertaining to births is not always available. As can be observed in Table 8.3, the total fertility rate for the years 1970 to 1990 is only available for West Malaysia because the required birth statistics for Sabah and Sarawak are not available. It was only in 1991 that the necessary birth statistics required for the computation of the rate for the whole of Malaysia were available, and hence the rate for 1991 to 2005 is presented in the bottom of the table.[11] The rate, published in the various official vital statistics reports, is given in only one decimal place for the years 1970 to 1998. Since the rate is usually subjected to very minor changes from year to year, two decimal places would be preferred to reveal the sensitive annual movements over the years, and also the differences in fertility levels among various sub-groups of the population.

In commenting on the figures for West Malaysia given in the upper portion of Table 8.3, we need to look at whether they can be utilised to represent the general fertility trends for the whole of Malaysia. In 1970 the total number of births for West Malaysia was 309,378, comprising 87.8 per cent of the total births in Malaysia. More importantly, the total fertility rate in 1991 for West Malaysia was 3.4, which was exactly the same as that for Malaysia. It would appear that the figures for West Malaysia can be used as a good approximation of the general fertility trends in the whole of the country.

The 1970s witnessed a continuous decline in fertility, down by some 20.4 per cent from 4.9 in 1970 to 3.9 in 1979. On account of the

TABLE 8.3
Total Fertility Rate, 1970–2003

Year	TFR	Percentage Change	Year	TFR	Percentage Change
West Malaysia					
1970	4.9	—	1981	3.9	0.0
1971	4.9	0.0	1982	3.8	−2.6
1972	4.7	−4.1	1983	3.7	−2.6
1973	4.4	−6.3	1984	3.8	+2.7
1974	4.4	0.0	1985	3.9	+2.6
1975	4.2	−4.5	1986	3.7	−5.1
1976	4.2	0.0	1987	3.5	−5.4
1977	4.0	−5.0	1988	3.6	+2.9
1978	3.9	−2.5	1989	3.2	−11.1
1979	3.9	0.0	1990	3.3	+3.1
1980	3.9	0.0	1991	3.4	+3.0
Malaysia					
1991	3.4	—	1999	3.07	−1.1
1992	3.5	+4.7	2000	2.88	−6.2
1993	3.5	0.0	2001	2.99	+3.8
1994	3.4	−2.9	2002	2.94	−1.6
1995	3.4	0.0	2003	2.90	−1.4
1996	3.3	−2.9			
1997	3.3	0.0			
1998	3.1	−6.1			

70-million policy, the 1980s failed to register a continuous decline as a slight rise even appeared in three years, resulting in a smaller reduction of 17.9 per cent during the second decade. A further slowdown in fertility decline amounting to only 8.0 per cent was experienced in the 1990s, though a slight rise was noticeable in one year. In 2000 fertility decreased by 6.2 per cent to reach the all-time low of 2.88, but it went up the next year to 2.99 and then fell again until 2003. In West Malaysia fertility has commenced to fall in the late 1950s, and this was probably true in the case of Malaysia though we do not have any total fertility rate to confirm this. Having started to fall years ago, it is not surprising that a deceleration in fertility decline occurred since 1970.

FERTILITY DIFFERENTIALS

In Malaysia the process of racial assimilation has taken place on such a minor scale that each ethnic group still retains its own basic traits as determined by diverse religions and cultural backgrounds. The earliest racial integration was known to have occurred in the early nineteenth century when some of the Chinese men, faced with a shortage of women from their own races, had taken Malay women as their wives. Their offspring, known as Straits-born Chinese or *Babas* tend to adopt Malay customs, language, attire and food, but very rarely the Muslim religion. Being mostly followers of Buddhism and Confucianism, their marriage and childbearing behaviour conforms closely to that of the Chinese population in general. In the course of time, however, most of their children showed an increasing tendency to take spouses from among the Chinese community and this early racial intermingling became negligible. A more enduring case refers to the South Indian Muslims who have assimilated with the Malays through a common religion and inter-marriage. They have fully integrated with the Malay community, but the vast majority of the South Indians have remained distinctly separate. The New Economic Policy (NEP) introduced in the 1970s has in fact exacerbated the segregation of the various ethnic groups in the country. In this kind of environment, an analysis of the differences in the fertility levels among the ethnic groups would be essential.

As shown in Table 8.4, the figures for the total fertility rate for the whole of Malaysia in respect of the three main ethnic groups are only available from 1991 onwards. The total fertility rate is the best measure of fertility level, and is therefore the most suitable index for the purpose of studying fertility differentials among the various sub-groups of the

TABLE 8.4
Total Fertility Rate by Ethnic Group, 1991–2003

Ethnic Group	Bumiputeras	Chinese	Indians	Chinese = 100	
				Bumiputeras	Indians
1991	4.2	2.5	2.8	168	112
1994	4.0	2.6	2.7	154	104
1999	3.64	2.17	2.58	168	119
2003	3.36	2.29	2.43	147	106

population. In 1991 the highest fertility was that of the Bumiputeras with a rate of 4.2, some 68 per cent higher than the rate of 2.5 for the Chinese. The 2.8 rate for the Indians was nearer to that of the Chinese, being only 12 per cent higher. This relative position of fertility levels among these three ethnic groups has persisted until today, and will probably continue to do in the years ahead. The higher fertility experienced by the Bumiputeras may be attributed to their lower average age at first marriage, the higher proportion of women ultimately married, and the lower level of birth control practice.[12]

The different regions of the country differ quite sharply in the degree of urbanisation, the extent of educational attainment, the type of economic activity, the level of socio-economic advancement, and the ethnic composition of the population. It is to be expected that these diverse conditions would lead to the presence of fertility differentials among the states as depicted in Table 8.5. The total fertility rate was on the high side in Kelantan (5.31), Trengganu (4.29), Perlis (3.45), and Kedah (3.41). These states in the northern portion of the Peninsula have relatively higher proportion of rural dwellers and Bumiputera population with a higher level of fertility.

In sharp contrast, the lower fertility was to be found in the eastern states of Penang (2.24), Selangor (2.31), Johore (3.02), Negri Sembilan (3.07), Malacca (3.22) and Perak (3.42). These states are more urbanised

TABLE 8.5
Total Fertility Rate by State, 2000

State	TFR	Penang = 100
Johore	3.02	135
Kedah	3.41	152
Kelantan	5.31	237
Malacca	3.22	144
Negri Sembilan	3.07	137
Pahang	3.30	147
Penang	2.24	100
Perak	3.42	153
Perlis	3.45	154
Selangor	2.31	103
Trengganu	4.29	192
Kuala Lumpur	2.30	103

and have a higher proportion of Chinese who experienced the lowest fertility among the major ethnic groups. The Federal Territory of Kuala Lumpur, while consisting of entirely urban dwellers, registered slightly higher fertility than Penang. This is due to the higher proportion of Chinese in this state than in Kuala Lumpur.

MORTALITY TRENDS

As in the case of fertility, the long-term trends in mortality will be examined in terms of three-year periods from 1970 onwards in order to reduce the fluctuation in the annual figures. In Table 8.6 are therefore given the annual average deaths and the crude death rates for three-year periods. The population denominator employed in the calculation of the crude death rate is taken as the average of the three mid-year populations in each of the three-year periods.

Except for the two periods from 1976 to 1981, the annual average number of deaths increased from 72,769 in 1970–1972 to 113,933 in the latest period 2002–2005. The rate of increase ranged from slightly below 1 per cent to about 10 per cent. It should however be emphasised that the rise in the number of births over the years was merely a reflection

TABLE 8.6
Annual Average Deaths and Crude Death Rates, 1970–2005

Period	Annual Average Deaths	Crude Death Rate	Percentage Change	
			Deaths	Rate
1970–1972	72,769	6.5	—	—
1973–1975	73,085	6.1	+0.4	−6.2
1976–1978	72,215	5.6	−1.2	−8.2
1979–1981	72,076	5.2	−0.2	−5.6
1982–1984	75,958	5.0	+5.4	−3.8
1985–1987	77,310	4.7	+1.8	−6.0
1988–1990	81,819	4.6	+5.8	−2.1
1991–1993	84,962	4.5	+3.8	−2.2
1994–1996	93,721	4.7	+10.3	+4.4
1997–1999	98,293	4.5	+4.9	−4.3
2000–2002	106,720	4.4	+8.6	−2.2
2003–2005	113,933	4.5	+6.8	+2.3

of the increasingly larger population as well as the ageing of the population. The crude death rate, on the other hand, followed a downward path. From a level of 6.5 per thousand population in the period 1970–1972, the crude death rate moved down to reach the low of 4.4 in 2000–2002, and then went up to 4.5 in the latest period. In the years ahead, there is a possibility that the crude death rate might display a gentle upward trend as the population continues to age.

The crude death rate is not a very good measure of overall mortality since it is distorted by the age structure of the population. An older population will invariably yield a higher crude death rate than a younger population. Despite the inherent shortcoming of the crude death rate, we can say that the general level of mortality during the last 35 years has been going downward. This long-term decline may be attributed to advances in medical knowledge, discovery of new drugs, better medical facilities, improved public hygiene and sanitation, and enhanced living conditions brought about by social and economic progress. Many tropical diseases, particularly malaria, that used to take a heavy toll of human lives were slowly but effectively brought under control.

Though the downtrend in overall mortality appeared to have been indicated by the crude death rate, it would be useful to study this mortality in terms of other more reliable indices. Table 8.7 presents the

TABLE 8.7
Infant and Neonatal Mortality Rates, 1970–2005

Period	Infant Mortality Rate	Neonatal Mortality Rate	Percentage Decline	
			I.M.R.	N.M.R.
1970–1972	37.5	21.0	—	—
1973–1975	34.2	20.4	8.8	2.9
1976–1978	28.1	16.4	17.8	16.4
1979–1981	22.9	13.8	18.5	15.9
1982–1984	19.0	11.9	17.0	13.8
1985–1987	15.5	10.0	18.4	16.0
1988–1990	13.6	8.7	12.3	13.0
1991–1993	12.0	7.8	11.8	10.3
1994–1996	10.1	6.6	15.8	15.4
1997–1999	8.4	5.3	16.8	19.7
2000–2002	6.8	4.5	19.0	15.1
2003–2005	5.4	3.7	20.6	17.8

infant mortality rate and the neonatal mortality rate for the same three-year periods from 1970 onwards. The infant mortality rate, defined as the number of deaths under one year of age per thousand live-births, is commonly accepted as a good index of mortality conditions prevailing in the country. The last 35 years have witnessed a relentless fall in this rate, being pushed down from 37.5 per thousand live-births in 1970–1972 to the record low of 5.4 in 2003–2005.

The level of infant mortality can be further analysed in terms of its two main components, viz., neonatal mortality and post-natal mortality. Neonatal mortality refers to deaths during the first four weeks of the morality infant life and post-natal to deaths during the remainder of the first year after birth. The latter is attributable to exogenous causes and is more amenable to environmental and medical controls, while the former is due to endogenous factors, which respond to these controls up to a point only. This is disclosed by the data provided in Table 8.7 where the reduction in the neonatal morality rate during every three-year period has been mostly smaller than that in the infant mortality rate. During the past 35 years, the path in neonatal mortality trend has been essentially downward all the way, dropping by 82.4 per cent from 21.3 in 1970–1972 to 3.5 in 2003–2005.

By far the most sophisticated technique of measuring overall mortality is by means of a life table based on a closed cohort of persons who are assumed to be subjected throughout their life to the death rates of the period. The figures for the life expectancy of a person at birth for each sex separately shown in Table 8.8 are obtained from various reports published by the Department of Statistics.[13] What is obvious is that the life expectancy at birth is always higher for the women than for men, a universal phenomenon that exists in all populations. In 1980 the life expectancy at birth for women was 71.0 years, 4.5 years or 6.8 per cent higher than that experienced by the men.

Another common feature of the data shown in the table refers to the improvement in life expectancy at birth enjoyed by both the women and men. From the initial 66.5 years in 1970, the life expectancy experienced by men was uplifted by 5.3 years or 8.0 per cent to reach 71.8 years in 2005. In the case of the women, their life expectancy was elevated from 71.0 years in 1980 to 76.2 years in 2005, up by 5.2 years or 7.3 per cent. As a result of the diverse movement recorded by the two sexes, the gap between the life expectancy at birth between men and women has narrowed to 4.4 years in 2005. The advance in life

TABLE 8.8
Life Expectancy By Sex, 1980–2005

Year	Male	Female	Year	Male	Female
1980	66.5	71.0	1993	69.4	73.8
1981	67.5	71.8	1994	69.4	74.0
1982	67.3	71.7	1995	69.4	74.2
1983	67.4	71.6	1996	69.3	74.3
1984	*	*	1997	69.6	74.6
1985	67.8	72.5	1998	69.7	74.7
1986	68.4	73.1	1999	69.9	75.0
1987	69.1	73.4	2000	70.0	74.6
1988	68.9	73.4	2001	70.2	75.2
1989	69.0	73.6	2002	70.2	75.6
1990	69.2	73.7	2003	71.1	75.6
1991	69.2	73.4	2004	71.7	76.1
1992	69.4	73.6	2005	71.8	76.2

* Not available.

expectancy experienced by both the men and women can be taken as a sure sign that overall mortality in the country has been lowered during the past 35 years or so.

MORTALITY DIFFERENTIALS

Apart from mortality under one year of age discussed earlier, it would be useful to study the variation in mortality level at the different ages. The age-specific death rates for each sex separately in respect of 2000 are presented in Table 8 9. In conformity with observations made in other countries, there is a distinct pattern of mortality over the whole age range. From the initial level in the first few years of life, mortality descends abruptly to the lowest level in the 5–9 age group, and then commences to climb gradually until the mid-forties, after which it rises progressively faster until the last survivor of the generation are extinguished.

For the men, the age-specific death rate commenced at 1.86 in the 0–4 age group, dropped suddenly to 0.37 in the 5–9 age group and then

TABLE 8.9
Age-Specific Death Rates by Sex, 2000

Age Group	Male	Female	M/F
0–4	1.86	1.56	119
5–9	0.37	0.26	143
10–14	0.46	0.29	159
15–19	1.25	0.32	391
20–24	1.59	0.52	306
25–29	1.80	0.56	321
30–34	2.15	0.74	291
35–39	2.75	1.11	248
40–44	3.74	1.92	195
45–49	4.96	2.82	176
50–54	8.51	5.26	162
55–59	13.11	8.18	160
60–64	23.68	14.68	161
65–69	34.45	24.27	142
70–74	52.60	40.04	131
75–79	88.93	77.44	115
80 & Over	139.43	120.10	116

moved up very gently to 3.74 in the 40–44 age group. Thereafter, it climbed up rapidly to touch the high of 139.43 in the last age group 80 and over. The women displayed a similar pattern, except that without any exception they experienced a lower mortality than the men throughout the whole age range. Another notable feature refers to the much higher mortality experienced by the men in the peak working age from 15 to 44, where the labour force participation rate of the men, very near 100 per cent, was much higher than that of the women. By and large, the mortality risk of the women homemakers was lower than those who worked. The mortality gap between the two sexes began to narrow progressively with the advanced old age when men began to retire from the workforce.

There has always been a variation in the mortality levels among the main ethnic groups in Malaysia. An idea of these ethnic mortality differentials is indicated in Table 8.10 showing the life expectancy at birth among each sex of the three main ethnic groups. An analysis of mortality differentials has assumed some significance viewed in the

TABLE 8.10

Life Expectancy at Birth by Sex and Ethnic Group, 1991–2004

Year	Bumiputeras	Chinese	Indians	Bumiputeras	
				Chinese	Indians
Male					
1991	68.8	70.7	64.2	102.8	93.3
1994	68.7	71.6	64.7	104.2	94.2
2000	69.0	72.0	65.5	104.3	94.9
2004	70.4	73.9	67.6	105.0	96.0
Female					
1991	71.9	76.4	71.4	106.3	99.3
1994	72.5	77.1	72.3	106.3	99.7
2000	73.3	77.6	73.6	105.9	100.4
2004	74.6	78.9	74.6	105.8	100.0

context of the New Economic Policy because such differentials are often regarded as pointers to the unbalanced social and economic progress that occurred among the major ethnic groups in the past. Indeed, the various five-year development plans have placed considerable emphasis on the improvement of medical and health programmes, particularly in the rural areas where the Bumiputera community dominate.

The general feature conveyed by the figures given in Table 8.10 is that the Chinese seemed to record the highest life expectancy at birth and the Indians the lowest, with the Malays occupying an intermediate position. In 1991 the life expectancy at birth was 70.7 years for the Chinese men, 68.8 years for the Bumiputera men and 64.2 years for the Indian men. This relative position was similar for the women, with 76.4 years, 71.9 years and 71.4 years respectively. By 2004 the Chinese men and women were still having the highest life expectancy, and the Bumiputera men and women the second highest.

Notes

1. Malaya, *Annual Report of the Family Planning Association of Selangor, 1958*.
2. Federation of Family Planning Associations, *History and Activities of the Federation of Family Planning Associations, Federation of Malaya, 1958–1965*. Ref. FFPA Gen. 24, Kuala Lumpur, 1965.

3. Saw Swee Hock, "Birth Control Use at Eve of the National Action Programme in West Malaysia", *Journal of Family Welfare* 16 (March 1970).

4. Malaysia, "Chapter XII: Health and Family Planning" in *First Malaysia Plan 1966–1970* (Kuala Lumpur: Government Press, 1965).

5. Malaysia, *Family, Planning Act 1966*, No. 42 of 1966, Warta Kerajaan: Seri Paduka Baginda. Kuala Lumpur, 12 May 1966.

6. See Mohamed Khir Johari, "National Family Planning Board: Chairman's Inaugural Address" and Abdul Razak bin Hussein, "Government Policy on Birth Control in' Malaysia", both in *Kajian Ekonomi Malaysia* 3, no. 1 (June 1966).

7. Nor Laily Aziz, *Malaysia: Population and Development* (Kuala Lumpur: National Family Planning Board, 1981).

8. The author, who was then Senior Lecturer in Statistics at the University of Malaya in Kuala Lumpur, was one of the members from the non-government sector.

9. Nor Laily Aziz, Tan Boon Ann, Ramli Othman and Kuan Lin Chee, *Facts and Figures: Malaysia National Population and Family Development* (Kuala Lumpur: National Family Planning Board, 1982).

10. The crude birth rate mentioned for the beginning of every five-year plan may appear inconsistent as compared to the actual rate attained in the last year of the previous plan, and this is due to the fact that a new five-year plan is prepared in advance of the expiry of the old one and hence the actual rate for the last year of the previous plan would not be available yet at that stage.

11. Malaysia, *Vital Statistics Time Series, Malaysia, 1963–1998* (Kuala Lumpur: Department of Statistics, 2001), and *Vital Statistics, Malaysia, 2003* (Kuala Lumpur: Department of Statistics, 2003).

12. Saw Swee Hock, *The Population of Peninsular Malaysia* (Singapore: Singapore University Press, 1988).

13. Malaysia, *Social Statistics Bulletin, Malaysia* (Kuala Lumpur: Department of Statistics, 2005).

9

Labour Force

The amount of labour available for the production of goods and services in a country is determined by a variety of demographic, social and economic factors. The size of the total population and its composition with respect to sex and age determine the maximum limits of the number of persons who can participate in economic activities. Other factors such as the race composition, the degree of urbanisation and the proportion of married women play an important part in influencing the proportion of the population, which will be represented in certain age groups in the working population. Among the more important economic and social factors are the industrial structure of the economy, the mode and organisation of production, the per capita income and the traditional attitudes towards working women and working children. By and large, demographic factors are the major determinants of the size of the male working population since by convention nearly all men are engaged in some form of gainful work from the time they reach adulthood until they approach the retirement age. On the other hand, socio-economic factors seem to exert a greater influence on the size of the female working population.

CONCEPTS AND DEFINITIONS

The labour force statistics of a country can be collected by means of the gainful worker approach or the labour force approach.[1] The older gainful worker concept was widely used before World War II and even during the early postwar years in some countries. In Peninsular Malaysia it was last used in September 1947 when the first postwar census of population was conducted. According to this concept the respondents were requested to state their usual occupation or gainful work from which they earned their income without reference to any time period. Those who were ascertained to have engaged in gainful work were considered as in the labour force, while those without any such work were classified as outside the labour force. Apart from the absence of a reference period to which the data could refer to, this method of collecting statistics cannot provide figures for the employed and the unemployed separately.

According to the labour force approach all respondents aged 10 years and over were asked to state whether they were working during the reference period, and if not, whether they were actively looking for work. Working is defined as being engaged in the production of goods and services. All those who were identified as working or actively looking for work were considered as economically active and included in the labour force, while the others were included in the economically inactive population. Persons enumerated as working constitute the employed, while those identified as not working but actively looking for work comprise the unemployed. The former group includes persons who were actually working during the reference period as well as persons who had a job but were temporarily laid off on account of sickness, leave, strike, bad weather, etc., and would be returning to work in due course. The employed group consists of persons who had worked previously and were looking for jobs during the reference period as well as those who had never worked before and were looking for jobs for the first time. Actively looking for work is defined as registering at an employment exchange, inserting and answering job advertisements, applying directly to prospective employers, making enquires from relatives and friends, or taking step to start one's own business.

The economically inactive population includes all persons who were not working and not actively looking for work during the reference period. Among the more important categories in the inactive population are those doing housework without pay, students, unpaid voluntary social workers, inmates of penal, mental or charitable institutions, retired persons, persons permanently disabled, persons deriving their income from rent, dividend, interest, etc., and all others not engaged in economic activities. It should be pointed out that among the economically inactive persons are those who have worked before and may re-enter the labour force in the future. But a much larger number, such as young students, would not have worked before and would enter the labour force for the first time in subsequent years.

Persons who were identified as economically active during the reference period were classified by employment status. This refers to the status of an individual with respect to his employment, that is, whether he is an employer, own account worker, unpaid family worker or employees. Employers refer to persons who operate either on their own or jointly with other partners a business, trade or profession and hire one or more employees, whereas those who do not engage any employees at all are known as own account workers. Employees refer to persons who work for individuals, firms or organisations and receive regular wages or salaries from them. Unpaid family workers refer to persons who assist in the family business, trade or enterprise without receiving any fixed wage or salary.

The labour force approach was utilised to collect and tabulate the statistics on the economically active population in the Population Censuses held once in ten years and the labour force survey conducted annually. In this chapter, we will use the statistics published annually in the Labour Force Survey Report to study the trends and structure of the labour force.[2] These statistics are preferred because they are available every year, and of course for the latest year 2004, instead of every ten years. Moreover, there is greater consistency in the presentation of these statistics in the series of annual reports than in the population censuses. For example, there was a radical departure in the presentation of the labour force statistics in the 2000 Census Report where the tables provide the figures in terms of employed persons only, and no figures for the labour force (employed and unemployed) were made available.[3]

LABOUR FORCE PARTICIPATION RATES

In the preceding section, we have observed the continuous growth in the labour force, though at an irregular pace. To ascertain whether this increase was caused solely by population growth or also by a rise in the extent of participation of the people in economic activity, we will proceed to study the labour force participation rate which, in our case, may be defined as the percentage of active persons aged 15 to 64 of the total population within the same age range. This rate serves to give an idea of the proportion of the population aged 15 to 64 who supply the labour on which the economic life of the country depends. The participation rate will be examined in terms of sex, citizenship, age and ethnic group.

In Table 9.1 we have presented the labour force participation rates
for the age group aged 15 to 64 by sex and citizenship computed from
data derived from the Labour Force Survey. The overall participation
rate for Malaysia stood at 64.9 per cent in 1980, fluctuated around this
level over the years, and ended at 64.4 in 2004. However, the participation
rates for males and females moved in the opposite direction. During the
whole period, the male rate moved down consistently from 85.9 per cent
to 80.9 per cent, while the female rate went up to 47.3 per cent from 44.0
per cent. As to be expected, the women participated in economic activity
to the extent of slightly more than half that of the men.

Since the non-citizens comprised mostly foreign workers admitted
into the country to work in the labour-shortage sectors of the economy,
the labour force participation rate of the non-citizens must necessarily
be higher than that of the citizens. This feature is confirmed by the
separate figures for the two categories of citizenship shown in the lower
section of the table. For example, the overall participation rate in 1995

TABLE 9.1

**Labour Force Participation Rates of Population
Aged 15–64 by Sex and Citizenship, 1980–2004**

Year	Total	Male	Female
		Total	
1980	64.9	85.9	44.0
1985	65.7	85.6	45.9
1990	66.5	85.3	47.8
1995	64.7	84.3	44.7
2000	65.4	83.0	47.2
2004	64.4	80.9	47.3
		Citizens	
1995	64.1	83.5	44.6
2000	63.7	81.4	45.8
2004	63.0	80.2	45.6
		Non-Citizens	
1995	77.2	97.0	47.1
2000	81.9	97.2	57.3
2004	81.7	96.3	62.1

was 77.2 per cent for the non-citizens as compared to the lower rate of 64.1 per cent for the citizens. This contrast in economic participation between citizens and non-citizens has persisted until today when the gap is even wider. The two respective rates were 81.7 per cent and 63.0 per cent. Similar figures for the years prior to 1995 are not made available in the annual report on the Labour Force Survey.

If we look at the male and female figures separately, the contrast in the participation rates also existed in all these years. In 2005 the participation rate for the male citizens was 80.2 per cent as compared to the higher rate of 95.3 per cent for the male non-citizens. A far more striking contrast was displayed by the women, the citizens registering a rate of 45.6 per cent in 2005 and the non-citizens a much higher rate of 62.1 per cent. While the higher skilled foreign workers are allowed to bring their wives, and children if any, into the country, the bulk of the foreign workers, being unskilled, are not permitted to do so. Female workers are admitted specifically to work, and hence the much higher participation rate among the female non-citizens.

It is known that the extent of participation in economic activity varies considerably among different age groups. To study this pattern of variation, we will use the age-specific labour force participation rate which may be defined as the percentage of economically active persons among the total population of a given age group. It is customary to calculate these rates of each sex separately in view of the traditional differences in the age participation rates between men and women at the various age groups. In Table 9.2 are prevailed the ratio for quinary age groups from 15 to 64 years, the two age cut-off points adopted in the annual Labour Force Survey.

A casual glance at the figures in Table 9.2 is sufficient to confirm the entirely different pattern of age-specific rates exhibited by each sex. Looking at the 1980 figures, we see the male rates rising steeply at the young ages to a shade above the 90 per cent level at early twenties and remains around the neighbourhood of 98 per cent through ages 25 to 49, after which it falls decisively as disabilities gradually remove men from the workforce. This general shape, which continued to prevail all these years, merely reflects the traditional attitude that unless a man is inflicted by ill health or permanently disabled he should work even though he may be a person of some wealth.

The female pattern differs in two important respects; the rates are appreciably lower at all ages and the progression of the curve follows

TABLE 9.2
Age-Specific Labour Force Participation Rates by Sex, 1980–2004

Age Group	1980	1985	1990	1995	2000	2004
Male						
15–19	50.9	46.9	47.3	37.9	32.3	27.8
20–24	92.6	91.8	90.1	89.5	85.4	78.0
25–29	97.9	98.3	97.7	97.9	67.6	96.2
30–34	98.5	98.9	98.6	98.3	98.7	98.3
35–39	98.2	99.1	98.8	98.6	98.7	98.2
40–44	98.4	98.5	98.5	98.0	98.2	97.8
45–49	97.6	98.0	97.5	97.2	97.9	97.3
50–54	94.9	93.9	93.5	93.6	93.6	92.6
55–59	81.4	77.8	72.7	73.4	75.2	72.6
60–64	72.0	69.6	62.6	62.0	61.6	60.0
Female						
15–19	34.2	31.4	33.8	26.8	21.9	18.2
20–24	54.6	57.9	63.3	61.1	61.5	56.6
25–29	55.9	49.5	53.3	52.8	59.9	63.9
30–34	43.7	47.7	50.4	49.0	53.3	57.9
35–39	47.0	49.4	48.9	49.2	51.2	54.1
40–44	49.0	52.2	50.1	47.6	52.2	52.2
45–49	48.3	50.2	50.3	45.3	49.7	51.9
50–54	44.1	42.7	43.1	36.9	40.6	43.6
35–59	35.7	35.1	33.1	27.4	28.5	32.3
60–64	28.3	26.3	27.0	21.5	23.2	22.2

quite a different path. From the young ages the rate rises to about 54.6 per cent in the early twenties and 55.9 per cent in the late twenties, and immediately dips to 43.7 per cent in the early thirties, then it rises again to reach the second but lower peak of 49.0 per cent in the early forties. Thereafter, the rate falls steadily to the early sixties. Withdrawal of women from the workforce on account of marriage or childbirth is responsible for the dip, while subsequent re-entry after the birth of the children, or after the children are older causes the second rise from the late thirties onwards. However, this female twin-peak curve has vanished in recent years partly because fewer women no longer withdraw from the workforce for the reasons stated and partly because of the replacement of women who actually withdraw by foreign female workers.

FIGURE 9.1

Age-Specific Labour Force Participation Rates, 1980 and 2005

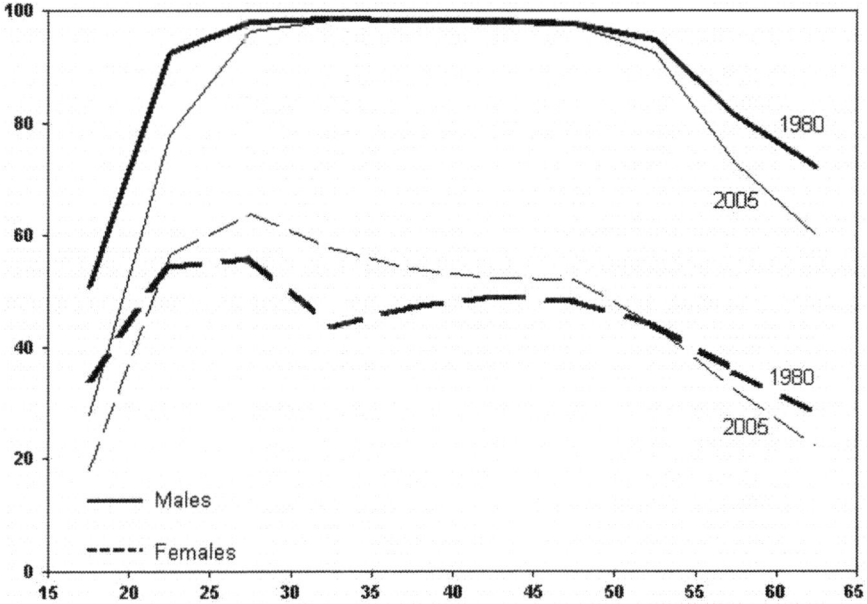

The broad shape of both the male rates and the female rates has remained somewhat similar over the years, though some changes were noticeable at certain ages at the two ends of the span of potentially active life. The last twenty-five years have witnessed a fall in the male rate from 50.9 per cent in the age group 15–19 to 27.8 per cent, so has the second age group 20–24 saw the rate dropped from 92.6 per cent to 78.0 per cent. In the case of the female rate, the drop only occurred in the first age group, down from 34.2 per cent to 18.2 per cent. At the other end of the age range, there was also a perceptible drop in the male rate in the last two groups aged 55 to 64, but this downward swing occurred in only the last age group 60–64 in the case of the female rate.

The above trends reflect, on the one hand, a rise in the average age at which young persons enter the labour force on account of prolongation of education, and on the other, a rising proportion of voluntary or involuntary retirement at the older ages. Either or both of these tendencies tend to compress men's, and to a lesser extent women's, working lives within a shorter age span have been observed in most countries in the neighbouring region. By and large, these countries have witnessed the growth of facilities and demand for secondary and tertiary education, the contraction of opportunities for self-employment and unpaid family work, the development of public and private pension schemes, and the rising levels of income, which have made possible for both more education of the young and earlier retirement of the old.

The data laid out in Table 9.3 illustrate the differences in the pattern of age-specific participation rates of the citizen population displayed by the main ethnic groups. It should be emphasised that the statistics made available in the annual Labour Force Survey in respect of ethnic groupings have adhered to the current practice of presenting the figures in terms of the citizen population rather than the total population (citizens and non-citizens combined). What this implies is that whatever picture unveiled by the figures will not be affected or distorted by the foreign workers within the non-citizen population. We would therefore be dealing with a more genuine portrayal of the differences in the participation rates of the major ethnic groups in the country.

In general, the differences have been more pronounced and interesting for the females than for the males, the working life of the latter being determined by economic consideration and that of the former by economic and family reasons such as marriage, childbearing and childcare, and household responsibilities. The Other Bumiputera men, being predominantly rural agricultural folks in Sabah and Sarawak, seemed to commence work at a relatively early age, 38.9 per cent in the 15–19 age group. The men that started work the latest were the highly urbanised Chinese with a corresponding figure of only 21.0 per cent. The great expansion of educational facilities for particularly the Bumiputeras in West Malaysia under the New Economic Policy has resulted in the Malay men staying in schools and universities and commencing work later. The participation rate in the 15–19 age group for Malay males was on the low side of 24.8 per cent. The participation rate for the Indian men in the same age group was even higher, 28.9 per cent.

With regard to the female rates, it is possible to pinpoint more differences in the pattern of participation rates among the ethnic groups. As in the case of the men, the relative starting time in the workforce as reflecting in the youngest age group 15–19 was quite

TABLE 9.3

Age-Specific Labour Force Participation Rates by Citizen Population by Sex and Ethnic Group, 2004

Age Group	Malays	Other Bumiputeras	Chinese	Indians	Others
			Male		
15–19	24.3	38.9	21.0	28.9	39.4
20–24	75.7	86.3	72.6	78.2	86.9
25–29	95.6	94.2	97.0	95.7	100.0
30–34	97.9	99.1	97.8	98.9	100.0
35–39	98.3	97.8	97.9	97.7	94.5
40–44	97.5	98.0	97.9	96.7	100.0
45–49	96.8	97.5	97.8	95.8	95.6
50–54	93.0	95.1	92.0	85.0	97.8
55–59	72.3	82.8	71.6	62.8	69.7
60–64	63.2	75.5	53.7	46.6	27.7
			Female		
15–19	15.8	23.2	13.8	16.4	62.5
20–24	54.6	46.6	60.4	60.6	68.7
25–29	61.9	42.8	77.0	62.9	55.5
30–34	56.4	48.3	65.4	53.5	49.3
35–39	52.1	53.0	56.6	52.9	69.5
40–44	52.1	54.0	48.3	55.6	47.2
45–49	51.7	61.4	50.1	43.7	58.8
50–54	44.5	54.3	41.1	33.9	48.8
55–59	32.1	59.5	28.7	13.7	59.4
60–64	21.7	51.7	17.7	8.5	57.6

similar, 23.2 per cent for Other Bumiputera women, 13.8 per cent for the Chinese women and 15 3 per cent for the Malay women. Greater contrasts are underlined by the figures for the old age groups. In the oldest age group 60–64, the highest participation rate was not surprisingly experienced by the Other Bumiputeras with 51.7 per cent. This level of participation in economic activities was nearly three times higher than that of the Chinese women with only 17.7 per cent. Even at the slightly less older age group 55–59, the level of economic participation of the Other Bumiputra women was more than twice that of the Chinese women. Another prominent difference refers to the peak of economic participation occurring in the 25–29 age group for the Malay women (61.9 per cent), in the 45–49 group for the Other Bumiputera women (61.4 per cent), and in the 25–29 age group for the Chinese women (77.0 per cent). It is worth mentioning that the difficulty of raising the level of economic participation of the various ethnic groups within the local or citizen population has necessitated the inflow of foreign workers, legal or illegal, from the neighbouring countries.

INDUSTRIAL STRUCTURE

The labour force of a country identified by means of the labour force approach is always classified according to industry and occupation. Industry is used to refer to the economic activity or the nature of business of the firm, establishment or department in which the person was employed during the reference week. The tabulation of the labour force by occupation serves to indicate the degree and nature in which division of labour is arranged, while the classification by industry serves to underline the integration of occupations and the type of units into which work is organised. By and large, an investigation into the industrial structure and occupational pattern of the labour force will reveal how the people of Malaysia are organised to earn their livelihood in the production of goods and services.

The data on industry were processed and tabulated according to the *Malaysia Standard Industrial Classification 2000* published by the Department of Statistics, which is based on the *International Standard Industrial Classification of All Economic Activities, Revision 3*, published by the United Nations. In analysing the long-term changes in the industrial structure of the labour force, we will look first at the data in terms of the following three broad sectors of economic activity:

1. Primary: agriculture, forestry, hunting and fishing.
2. Secondary: mining, manufacturing, construction, electricity, gas and water.
3. Tertiary: commerce, transport, storage, communications and services.

Broadly speaking, the trends in the percentage of the labour force by the above three sectors would give us an idea of the past changes that have taken place in the economy.[+] To examine this aspect of the labour force, we will use the statistics collected in the Labour Force Survey to provide some consistency and hence comparability in our analysis.

The data laid out in Table 9.4 show that the number of employed persons in the primary sector has undergone ups and downs in the last twenty-five years. Starting from 1,780,600 in 1980, it went down and up regularly every five years, and finally to the lower figure of 1,511,100 towards the end of the period in 2004. The secondary sector witnessed a continuous growth from 1,154,300 in 1980 to 2,972,600 in 2005, an increase of some 157.5 per cent. A more remarkable growth was registered by the tertiary sector whose share of the employed persons was raised from 1,852,400 in 1980 to 5,502,900 in 2004, an increase of about 197.1 per cent.

As a result of the above changes a swing away from employment in the primary sector has taken place over the last twenty-five years. The proportion employed in the primary sector fell from 27.2 per cent in 1980 to only 15.1 per cent in 2004. Accompanying this swing was the consistent rise in the relative importance of the service sector, moving up from 38.7 per cent to 55.1 per cent during the whole period. The proportion in the secondary sector did not display any clear trend, fluctuating from the initial 24.1 per cent to reach the slightly higher level of 29.8 in 2004. The shift in the relative importance of the three broad

TABLE 9.4

Distribution of Employed Persons Aged 15–64
by Three Broad Sectors of Economic Activity, 1980–2004

Sector	1980	1985	1990	1995	2000	2004
	Number ('000)					
Primary	1,780.6	1,717.4	1,832.5	1,526.8	1,711.8	1,511.1
Secondary	1,154.3	1,345.7	1,621.7	2,472.3	3,000.1	2,972.6
Tertiary	1,852.4	2,590.2	2,936.7	3,645.8	4,609.8	5,502.9
Total	4,787.3	5,653.3	6,390.9	7,645.0	9,321.7	9,986.6
	Percentage					
Primary	27.2	30.4	28.7	20.0	18.4	15.1
Secondary	24.1	23.8	25.4	32.3	32.2	29.8
Tertiary	38.7	45.8	45.9	47.7	49.4	55.1
Total	100.0	100.0	100.0	100.0	100.0	100.0

sectors should be viewed in terms of the emphasis on the production of primary products in the early years, subsequent diversification programmes based on industrialisation, and the more recent growth in services as the economy adjusted to globalisation influences.

A greater insight into the current industrial structure of the workforce can be observed in Table 9.5 showing nine major industrial groups in terms of sex, citizen and urban/rural area. According to the first column of the table, the sector providing the greatest job opportunities in 2004 was manufacturing, absorbing some 20.3 per cent of the total employed persons. The second with 16.1 per cent was the group known as wholesale and retail trade, repair of motor vehicles, motorcycles, and personal and household goods. Agriculture, hunting and forestry, though important in the past, has been reduced to third position, providing jobs to about 13.5 per cent. The relative importance of the other eleven industrial groups did not vary significantly, except that electricity, gas and water sector took in only 0.6 per cent and mining and quarrying 0.3 per cent.

We will now proceed to look at the interesting variation in the industrial structure of the workplace between the two sexes. The top three sectors for the male workers were manufacturing (18.9 per cent), wholesale and retail trade, repair of motor vehicles, motorcycles, and personal and household goods (16.5 per cent), and agriculture, hunting and forestry (15.1 per cent). The first two sectors also featured as the top two for the female workers, but the third spot was replaced by education, health and social work. Indeed, it is quite common to have a much larger proportion of the female workers (14.5 per cent) than the male workers (4.5 per cent) in education, health and social work. A similar situation prevailed in private households with employed persons, which offered jobs to 6.8 per cent of the female workers, but only 0.2 per cent to male workers. Most of the women worked as domestic maids. A very much higher proportion of the men (12.9 per cent) were employed in the construction industry as compared to the women (1.8 per cent). The transport, storage and communications sector exhibited a similar, though less pronounced, pattern with 7.0 per cent of the men and only 2.2 per cent of the women.

We have observed the recent influx of foreign workers, and it would be interesting to see in what sectors of the economy they were employed. The non-citizens, consisting primarily these foreign workers, were concentrated in agriculture, hunting and fishing with 29.5 per cent. Most of them were working in the agricultural estates such as oil palm and rubber plantations. The second most popular sector where the non-

TABLE 9.5

Percentage Distribution of Employed Persons Aged 15–64 by Industry, Sex, Citizenship and Urban/Rural Area, 2004

	Industry	Total	Sex		Citizenship		Urban/Rural	
			Male	Female	Citizens	Non-Citizens	Urban	Rural
1.	Agriculture, hunting and forestry	13.5	15.1	10.6	11.7	29.5	2.4	33.6
2.	Fishing	1.3	2.0	0.1	1.3	1.3	0.7	2.4
3.	Mining and quarrying	0.3	0.5	0.1	0.3	0.7	0.3	0.4
4.	Manufacturing	20.3	18.9	22.8	20.1	22.0	21.6	17.9
5.	Electricity, gas and water	0.6	0.8	0.2	0.6	0.0	0.7	0.4
6.	Construction	8.9	12.9	1.8	8.6	11.8	9.8	7.4
7.	Wholesale and retail trade; repair of motor vehicles, motorcycles, personal and household goods	16.1	16.5	15.4	16.9	8.3	19.3	10.3
8.	Hotels and restaurants	7.0	5.5	9.6	7.3	4.5	7.8	5.5
9.	Transport, storage and communications	5.3	7.0	2.2	5.7	1.7	6.2	3.7
10.	Financing, insurance, real estate and business activities	6.9	6.0	8.1	7.5	2.0	9.2	2.7
11.	Public administration and defence; compulsory social security	6.8	7.8	5.1	7.5	0.5	7.5	5.6
12.	Education, health and social work	8.1	4.5	14.5	8.8	1.4	8.4	7.6
13.	Other community, social and personal service activities	2.3	2.1	2.7	2.4	1.4	2.8	1.5
14.	Private households with employed persons	2.6	0.2	6.8	1.2	15.0	3.4	1.1
	Total	100.0	100.0	100.0	100.0	100.0	100.0	100.0

citizens were fond of working was manufacturing which took in some 22.0 per cent. The other unique feature concerns the high of some 15.0 per cent of the non-citizens in private households with employed persons. This encompassed mainly foreign women working as domestic maids in these households; only 1.2 per cent of the citizens are employed here. As compared to the citizens, a very small proportion of the non-citizens were to be found in public administration and defence, and compulsory social security (0.5 per cent) and in education, health and social work (1.4 per cent).

Another noteworthy aspect of the labour force is the one concerning the industrial distribution in the urban and the rural areas as portrayed in Table 9.5. In the urban area, the manufacturing sector provided jobs to the largest group of workers (21.6 per cent), followed closely by the 19.3 per cent in wholesale and retail trade, repair of motor vehicles, motorcycles, personal, and household goods. Not surprisingly, only a small proportion equivalent to 2.4 per cent in the urban area were employed in the agriculture, hunting and forestry sector. In sharp contrast, their counterparts in the rural area had 33.6 per cent in this sector.

The constant attention given to the pattern of economic activities of the main ethnic groups in the country requires us to pay great attention to the industrial structure of the workforce among these groups. According to the data laid out in Table 9.6, the greatest concentration of the Malay workforce was in the manufacturing sector (20.9 per cent), followed way behind by wholesale and related trade; repair of motor vehicles, motorcycles, personal and household goods (11.8 per cent). Almost the similar proportion of Malay workforce was to be found in the public administration and defence; compulsory social security (11.6 per cent) and agricultural, hunting and forestry (10.9 per cent). Interestingly, the Other Bumiputeras did not display a similar industrial pattern. Being primarily indigenous peoples living in the rural parts of Sabah and Sarawak, they were heavily engaged in agriculture, hunting and forestry (35.3 per cent).[5] Only 10.5 per cent of their workforce were employed in the manufacturing sector.

By comparison, a very large proportion of the Chinese were employed in whole and retail trade; repair of motor vehicles, motorcycles, personal and household goods (29.0 per cent). They were fairly represented in manufacturing (19.8 per cent), construction (12.0 per cent), and financing, insurance, real estate and business activities (10.1 per cent). The Chinese have of course played a dominant role in the business sector of the

TABLE 9.6

Percentage Distribution of Employed Citizens Aged 15–64 by Industry and Ethnic Group, 2004

	Industry	Malays	Other Bumiputeras	Chinese	Indians	Others
1.	Agriculture, hunting and forestry	10.9	35.3	5.2	6.4	17.4
2.	Fishing	1.3	2.8	1.0	0.1	0.6
3.	Mining and quarrying	0.3	0.6	0.2	0.2	0.8
4.	Manufacturing	20.9	10.5	19.8	29.5	16.4
5.	Electricity, gas and water	0.8	0.8	0.1	1.4	0.0
6.	Construction	7.4	7.2	12.0	5.8	11.4
7.	Wholesale and retail trade; repair of motor vehicles, motorcycles, personal and household goods	11.8	10.6	29.0	15.2	17.4
8.	Hotels and restaurants	8.0	4.5	7.9	4.2	8.1
9.	Transport, storage and communications	5.8	4.3	4.7	11.2	3.3
10.	Financing, insurance, real estate and business activities	6.6	3.1	10.1	9.6	9.4
11.	Public administration and defence; compulsory social security	11.6	9.0	0.9	4.0	1.3
12.	Education, health and social work	8.3	8.8	6.2	3.7	4.8
13.	Other community, social and personal service activities	4.8	4.2	3.8	6.1	4.2
14.	Private households with employed persons	1.1	1.0	1.3	1.4	5.9
	Total	100.0	100.0	100.0	100.0	100.0

economy. It should also be noted that an extremely small proportion of
the Chinese workforce was involved in public administration and defence;
compulsory social security (0.9 per cent). This may be partly attributed
to the government policy of according job preferences in the civil service
and defence to Bumiputeras. The Chinese being essentially urban dwellers,
have a relatively small proportion working in agriculture, hunting and
forestry (5.2 per cent).

By comparison, the Indians have a slightly higher proportion in
agriculture, hunting and forestry (6.4 per cent), but they are mostly
plantation workers rather than farmers. The more noteworthy feature is
that they have a bigger proportion working in manufacturing (29.5 per
cent) and storage, transport and communications (11.2 per cent). However,
being also affected by the job preferential treatment for Bumiputeras,
the Indians have a relatively low proportion in public administration and
defence; compulsory social security (4.0 per cent).

OCCUPATIONAL PATTERNS

Having examined in some detail the industrial structure of the labour
force, we will proceed to study the equally important aspect of the
labour force in terms of occupational classification. The occupation of a
person refers to the trade or profession followed or the type of work
performed during the reference week. Tabulation of the labour force by
occupation presents both an inventory of skills possessed by a country
at any point in time and useful information on the rate of development
of a country. Changes in occupational pattern provide some indication of
the social mobility of the people consequent on enhanced educational
attainment and increased economic opportunities. In some respects, the
occupation of a person also serves as a measure of his social status in
society and its reflection of his earning capacity.

The data on occupation collected in the Labour Force Survey were
processed and tabulated according to the *Malaysia Standard Classification
of Occupation 1998* published by the Department of Statistics, which was
based on the *International Standard Classification of Occupations (ISCO-
88)* published by the United Nations. The classification has been designed
to present information on occupation in descending order of detail
according to the one-digit, two-digit or three-digit levels. However, we
will use mostly data at the one-digit level. The data refer to persons who
were working during the reference, and exclude those who unemployed

during the week, regardless whether they were first-timers or had worked previously.

In Table 9.7 we have presented the employed persons in 2004 according to sex, citizenship and urban/rural area. The data reveals the existence of pronounced differences in the occupational pattern between the male and female workers. The three most popular occupational groups for the men were plant and machine operators and assemblers (15.7 per cent), craft and related trade workers (15.4 per cent), and skilled agricultural and fishery workers (15.0 per cent). The women, on the other hand, were to be found in completely different three top occupational groups These three groups were service workers and shop and market sales (13.4 per cent), clerical workers (17.9 per cent), and technicians and associate professionals (13.0 per cent). Another interesting feature refers to the marked contrast in two occupational groups between the men and women. Only 5.9 per cent of female workers were engaged as legislators, senior officials and managers as compared to 10.1 per cent for the male workers. A more striking divergence was underlined by the 17.5 per cent for women and 4.7 per cent for men in the clerical group.

Countries confronted with a shortage of labour depend heavily on the import of foreigners to work particularly in certain occupations where locals tend to avoid. In such countries we can expect a completely different type of occupational pattern to be displayed by the local workers and the foreign workers.[6] There are no precise statistics available for us to study this aspect of the labour force in Malaysia, but a good proxy can be provided by the data for the citizen labour force and the non-citizen labour force, which would include mostly foreign workers. Table 9.7 shows that a shade more than half of the non-citizen employed persons were centred on two occupational groups. Some 27.8 per cent were engaged in elementary occupations such as domestic maids and unskilled manual labourers. The other 26.6 per cent were working as skilled agricultural and fishery workers, especially in the rubber and oil palm plantations. The non-citizens registered a very low proportion in clerical workers (0.7 per cent) and technicians and associate professionals (2.7 per cent). The two respective proportions for the citizens were 10.2 per cent and 13.1 per cent.

Another interesting aspect of the labour force depicted in the table refers to the difference in the occupational pattern of the employed persons in the urban and rural areas. As to be expected, an exceptionally large proportion of the workers in the rural area were skilled agricultural

TABLE 9.7

Percentage Distribution of Employed Persons Aged 15–64 by Sex, Citizenship and Urban/Rural Area, 2004

Occupation	Sex			Citizenship		Urban/Rural	
	Total	Male	Female	Citizens	Non-Citizens	Urban	Rural
1. Legislators, senior officials and managers	8.6	10.1	5.9	9.2	3.2	10.9	4.3
2. Professionals	5.6	4.9	6.7	5.9	2.6	7.2	2.6
3. Technicians and associate professionals	12.1	11.6	13.0	13.1	2.7	13.9	8.9
4. Clerical workers	9.3	4.7	17.9	10.2	0.7	11.8	4.7
5. Service workers and shop and market sales	14.8	12.8	18.4	15.5	8.3	16.8	11.2
6. Skilled agricultural and fishery workers	13.2	15.0	10.0	11.7	26.6	2.5	32.5
7. Craft and related trade workers	11.7	15.4	5.2	11.8	11.2	12.4	10.5
8. Plant and machine operators and assemblers	14.1	15.7	11.4	13.8	16.9	13.6	15.0
9. Elementary occupations	10.1	9.9	12.0	8.8	27.8	10.9	10.3
Total	100.0	100.0	100.0	100.0	100.0	100.0	100.0

TABLE 9.8

Percentage Distribution of Employed Citizens Aged 15–64 by Ethnic Group, 2004

	Industry	Malays	Other Bumiputeras	Chinese	Indians	Others
1.	Legislators, senior officials and managers	7.9	2.4	19.0	12.0	11.2
2.	Professionals	5.3	2.4	6.3	4.5	2.8
3.	Technicians and associate professionals	13.3	9.1	12.1	14.5	4.2
4.	Clerical workers	6.2	3.8	3.9	5.4	2.0
5.	Service workers and shop and market sales	13.9	10.8	14.1	12.2	15.2
6.	Skilled agricultural and fishery workers	13.3	33.8	6.3	3.5	19.2
7.	Craft and related trade workers	12.2	13.8	23.4	10.0	16.1
8.	Plant and machine operators and assemblers	16.8	14.0	10.2	25.8	15.4
9.	Elementary occupations	11.1	10.0	4.8	12.0	13.7
	Total	100.0	100.0	100.0	100.0	100.0

and fishery workers, 32.5 per cent in sharp contrast to 2.5 per cent in the urban area. On the reverse side, the rural workers had only 2.6 per cent employed in the professional occupation as compared to the 7.2 per cent for the urban workers. The other noticeable difference may be observed in clerical workers, which constituted 11.8 per cent of the urban workers but only 4.7 per cent of the rural worker.

In a multiracial society like that in Malaysia, it would be useful to analyse the differences in the occupational pattern of the main ethnic groups since there has always been some specialisation along ethnic lines. In interpreting this type of data presented in Table 9.8, we should bear in mind the possible impact of New Economic Policy according job preferences to Bumiputeras in the public sector and requiring companies to reserve a certain quota of jobs for Bumiputeras in the private sector.

By far the most noticeable highlight featured in the table was the exceptionally high proportion of the Other Bumiputeras employed as skilled agricultural and fishery workers (33.8 per cent). Most of them belong to the indigenous peoples working as farmers in the rural area and fishermen along riverine banks and coastal regions. A less lop-sided pattern, with proportions slightly above 11 per cent employed in six occupational groups, was displayed by the Malays. A completely different, but somewhat more lop-sided, occupational pattern was experienced by the Chinese workers. A relatively high proportion of the employed Chinese were working as legislators, senior officials and managers (19.0 per cent) as compared to only 2.4 per cent for the Other Bumiputeras and 7.9 per cent for the Malays. Only 6.3 per cent of the Chinese workers were engaged as skilled agricultural and fishery workers. The Indian workers were concentrated in two occupational groups, 25.8 per cent working as plant and machine operators and assemblers and 14.5 per cent as technicians and associate professionals.

Notes

1. For a discussion of these two concepts, see *United Nations, Handbook of Population Census Methods, Volume 11: Economic Characteristics of Population.* Series F, No. 5, Rev. 1, Studies in Method (New York, 1958).

2. Malaysia, *Labour Force Survey Report,* for years 1980–2005 (Kuala Lumpur: Department of Statistics).

3. Shaari bin Abdul Rahman, *2000 Population and Housing Census of Malaysia, Economic Characteristics of the Population* (Kuala Lumpur: Department of Statistics, 2003).

4. Saw Swee-Hock, 'The Structure of the Labour Force in Malaya", *International Labour Review* 98, no. 1 (July 1968).

5. Saw Swee-Hock, 'Regional Differences in the Structure of the Labour Force in Malaysia", *Kajian Ekonomi Malaysia* 3, no. 2 (December 1966).

6. Saw Swee-Hock, "Population and Labour Force Growth and Patterns in ASEAN Countries", *Philippine Review of Economies and Business* 25, nos. 3 & 4 (September and December 1988).

10

Future Population Trends

In this final chapter we will make an attempt to examine the most plausible course of future trends in the population of Malaysia. This can be accomplished by projecting the population into the future on the basis of certain assumptions concerning the future path of migration, mortality and fertility. Before analysing the salient features of these projected figures, we will discuss the 1984 pronatalist policy that has exerted some influence on the course of population dynamics in the country.

THE 70 MILLION POLICY

Many of the past demographic trends and patterns discussed earlier were influenced by government attitudes and policies, some of which are translated into administrative procedures or even enshrined in the laws of the country. In general, the future population trends will depend partly on what had already happened to the growth factors of fertility, mortality and migration in the immediate past and partly on government policies that are likely to affect the future path of population growth. In this respect, Malaysia stands out as one of the very few countries that are now advocating for a larger population than what was previously thought to be desirable and have even pin-pointed a particular population size to be achieved ultimately in the future.

The genesis of the new policy can be traced to September 1982 when the Prime Minister, Datuk Seri Dr Mahathir Mohamad, first mooted the idea of an ultimate population size of 70 million in his presidential address to a general assembly of the United Malay National Organisation (UMNO). His rationale was that Malaysia needs a big population to provide a large domestic market to support its future industries in the face of an increasingly protectionist world market. The concept of a large population was in sharp contradiction to the existing population policy under which the government family planning programme has been functioning for many years since 1966. It is not surprising that this sudden pronouncement sparked off considerable controversies and discussions about the implications of 70 million people in the fields of housing, education, health, employment, food production, water requirements and energy consumption.[1] Some of the ensuing debates were rather confusing in the face of a failure to provide reasons for selecting 70 million and to specify the year in which this target is to be attained.

It was no surprise that the government established in January 1983 an *ad hoc* Committee on Population Issues to study the strategy and programme required to achieve the 70 million target. The terms of reference of the Committee were (a) to review the present population growth trends and prospects, (b) to prepare population projections based on several assumptions leading towards achieving 70 million population, (c) to study some social and economic implications of 70 million, and (d) to make recommendations.[2] By the second quarter of 1984 the Prime Minister was able to use information supplied by this Committee to provide more details about the new population policy in his presentation of the mid-term review of the Fourth Five-Year Plan, 1981–85 in Parliament in April 1984. He announced that the aim of the policy is to achieve a population of 70 million in the year 2100.[3]

The report of the Committee was completed in mid-1984 and was approved by the Cabinet on 1 August 1984. It recommended that the present rate of decline in fertility should be decelerated in order to delay the attainment of replacement fertility level to the year 2070. In this manner the target of 70 million would be reached during the year 2100, and the population is expected to grow slightly to stabilise at about 73 million by the year 2150. The report assured that the social and economic implications of the 70 million population should not be alarming since this size would only be attained in approximately 115 years' time. To slow down the downward movement in fertility, the report recommended the introduction of measures that would encourage a large family size.

The first pronatalist measure introduced by the government was connected to the question of paid maternity leave for female workers. The *Employment (Amendment) Act, 1984* was passed by Parliament to extend the eligibility for paid maternity leave for women working in the public service from the first three to the first five births with effect from 1 June 1984.[4] Many female workers in the private sector have also benefited from this new maternity leave scheme since the working conditions in the private sector tend to fall in line with those provided by the government.

The second pronatalist measure involved changes in the amount of child relief allowed in the annual income tax assessment. In presenting the 1985 budget to Parliament on 19 October 1984, the Finance Minister announced that the total amount of child relief in the income tax returns for the first five children would be raised from $3,000 to $3,800.[5] The amount for each of these children was modified as follows:

Birth Order	Old	New
First	$800	$650
Second	$700	$750
Third	$600	$800
Fourth	$500	$800
Fifth	$400	$800

By comparison, the new scheme penalises parents with only one child, and even those with only two since the combined allowance is reduced from $1,500 to $1,400. But they will be able to enjoy an increasingly larger allowance when they produce their third, fourth and fifth child.[6]

In March 1985 the government introduced another pronatalist measure whereby female employees in the public service are now given maternity allowances up to the fifth birth instead of for the first three only.[7] In the private sector employers are required by government regulations to pay maternity allowance for the first four rather than the first two births only.

The pronatalist policy created problems for the National Family Planning Board, which has been spearheading the country's population control programme since 1966. It became apparently clear that the whole philosophy, function and operational programme of the Board had to be modified. For one thing, the name of the Board was no longer consistent with the new policy and was accordingly changed to National Population and Family Development Board. This was accompanied by a shift in the Board's original objective. Family planning is no longer meant to limit the ultimate size of the family but to space the birth of children in the interest of the health of the mother and the general welfare of the family. In fact, parents are now urged to produce more children instead of stopping at two.

In December 2004, it was announced in the Senate that Malaysia has decided to abandon its target for a population of 70 million in 2100 and would be placing more emphasis on having quality citizens and a caring society.[8] The Senate was informed that it was difficult to achieve the target within the timeframe due to several factors, including the rapid decline in fertility.

POPULATION PROJECTIONS

The population statistics classified by ethnic groups, as noted previously, being made available for the citizen population only implies that the population projections for the three main ethnic groups must necessarily be computed in terms of the citizen population and not the total population. The projections for each of the three main ethnic groups or the citizen population were prepared by the component method which involves the separate projections of the number of males and females in each age group of the population. We usually project the population by time-intervals equal to the age-intervals into which it has been divided. Since the 2000 base population has been divided into quinary age groups, the projections are most easily made for five-year intervals of time. This implies that at the end of a five-year period all the survivors of one age group would have moved into the next higher age group.[9]

Each cohort of the sex-age group is diminished to account for mortality with the passage of time. This step requires a set of five-year survival ratios which are deemed to represent mortality in each cohort during specific periods of time subsequent to 2000. A multiplication of the original number in each sex-age group by the relevant ratios will yield the estimated number of persons five years older at a date five years later in 2005. A repetition of the procedure will furnish the estimated population aged ten years older than those at the base date and for a date ten years later.

In the second step we are concerned with the estimation of the future number of children born in each five-year time interval subsequent to the base date in order to fill in the vacuum in the age group 0–4 at periods of time every five years later. To begin with, we need to formulate the most plausible assumption regarding the future course of fertility in terms of the age-specific fertility rates. These rates are then utilised in conjunction with the female population in the relevant reproductive age groups to derive the estimated number of births for the various five-year periods. The number of births surviving to the end of a given five-year period can be estimated by multiplying the number of births during the period with the appropriate survival ratio.

Another step would be required if international migration is taken into consideration in the computation. However, since we shall be assuming that no immigration and emigration will occur during the whole period of the projection, the procedure normally used to take migration into account need not be discussed here.

The results of any population projection depends primarily on the assumptions adopted in regard to migration, morality and fertility. It may be recalled that immigration from overseas countries is now under very rigid control, while emigration to these countries will probably continue to be negligible in the future. It was therefore decided to assume that migration will not exact a significant influence on future population trends. We have observed that, though falling continuously in the past, mortality has not touched the bottom point and can continue to fall further in the future. In our computation we have therefore assumed that mortality will continue to decline. Fertility, which has been declining in the past, is also assumed to decline in the future. But the fertility decline in each of the three major races has been assumed to decline rather slowly in view of the 70 million policy.

The assumption used to compute the projections for each of the three main ethnic groups within the citizen population in Malaysia may be summarised as follows:

Migration

For every ethnic citizen population, it is assumed that the population is a closed one not subject to external migration.

Mortality

For the Bumiputera citizen population, it is assumed that the 2005 mortality level with a life expectancy at birth of 71.7 years will improve regularly during the whole projection period to reach 79.5 years in 2035.

For the Chinese citizen population, it is assumed that the 2005 mortality level with a life expectancy at birth of 75.0 years will improve to 79.5 years in 2020 and remain at the level up to 2035.

For the Indian citizen population, it is assumed that the 2005 mortality level with a life expectancy at birth of 70.2 years will improve regularly to reach 78.0 years in 2035.

Fertility

For the Bumiputera citizen population, it is assumed that fertility will decline by 2 per cent every five years from the initial total fertility rate of 3.28 in 2005 to reach 2.91 in 2035.

For the Chinese citizen population, it is assumed that fertility will decline by 2 per cent every five years from the initial total fertility rate of 2.27 in 2005 to reach 2.05 in 2035.

For the Indian citizen population, it is assumed that fertility will decline by 2 per cent every five years from the initial total fertility rate of 2.41 in 2005 to reach 2.13 in 2035.

The results of the projections for the citizen population of the three main ethnic groups by sex and quinary age group are presented in Tables 10.1 to 10.3.

FUTURE POPULATION GROWTH

It may be recalled that we have prepared population projections by sex and quinary age group for the three main ethnic groups and not for the total population of Malaysia. The total population has been calculated in two stages. The first stage notes that the combined citizen population of the three main ethnic groups amounted to 98.72 per cent of the total citizen population and the remaining 1.28 per cent consisted of the minority communities lumped together as Others. Assuming that the proportion of Others will remain constant throughout the projection period, we boost up the combined projected total of the three main ethnic groups by 1.28 per cent to give us the total citizen population.

In the second stage, we note that in 2005 the proportion of citizen population was 93.24 per cent, and the other 6.76 per cent consisted of non-citizen population. The projected total population for Malaysia (citizens and non-citizens) for every five years from 2010 to 2035 was obtained by boosting the total citizen population derived in the first

TABLE 10.1
Projected Bumiputera Citizen Population
by Sex and Age Group, 2005–2035

Age Group	2005	2010	2015	2020	2025	2030	2035
				Male			
0–4	915.2	1,060.9	1,184.1	1,284.7	1,334.5	1,310.4	1,301.8
5–9	953.5	911.0	1,057.3	1,181.4	1,282.0	1,331.9	1,307.9
10–14	963.3	951.7	909.7	1,056.2	1,180.3	1,280.9	1,330.8
15–19	901.6	961.1	950.0	908.4	1,054.8	1,178.7	1,279.5
20–24	792.9	898.4	958.6	948.3	906.9	1,053.1	1,177.0
25–29	617.0	789.5	895.4	956.0	945.9	904.7	1,050.7
30–34	531.2	613.8	786.0	892.0	952.8	942.9	902.0
35–39	484.8	527.5	561.0	781.9	887.6	948.2	938.6
40–44	478.9	479.8	522.6	604.9	775.5	880.6	940.9
45–49	416.6	471.0	472.7	515.5	597.3	766.1	870.1
50–54	324.9	405.2	459.4	461.9	504.4	585.2	750.8
55–59	247.3	310.5	388.7	442.1	445.7	487.7	566.1
60–64	164.3	229.9	296.2	364.6	415.7	420.2	460.0
65–69	133.3	146.1	205.6	266.4	329.3	376.4	381.5
70–74	74.5	110.3	121.8	172.5	224.7	278.8	319.6
75 & Over	100.3	116.9	155.6	190.8	253.8	335.6	431.8
Total	8,099.6	8,983.6	9,973.7	11,027.6	12,091.2	13,081.4	14,009.1
				Female			
0–4	856.8	993.8	1,108.9	1,204.1	1,263.3	1,227.7	1,219.0
5–9	898.0	853.6	991.1	1,107.6	1,203.0	1,262.3	1,272.4
10–14	909.6	896.7	852.8	990.5	1,106.8	1,202.4	1,261.7
15–19	863.1	908.0	895.5	851.8	989.6	1,105.8	1,201.5
20–24	782.2	860.8	906.2	894.1	850.6	988.3	1,104.4
25–29	624.0	779.6	858.5	904.2	892.3	849.1	986.6
30–34	549.7	621.3	776.7	855.8	901.5	889.9	846.9
35–39	519.3	546.5	618.1	773.0	851.7	897.5	886.1
40–44	483.7	514.9	542.3	613.5	767.3	845.9	891.4
45–49	409.4	477.3	508.7	536.0	606.6	759.0	837.2
50–54	314.1	400.9	468.0	500.3	528.4	598.4	748.9
55–59	237.4	304.0	388.7	451.3	483.5	511.4	579.9
60–64	160.5	225.4	289.1	371.1	432.0	463.7	491.3
65–69	145.5	147.1	207.2	266.5	342.7	399.9	430.0
70–74	87.4	125.2	127.5	180.3	232.2	299.1	349.2
75 & Over	120.1	147.0	196.8	232.8	299.0	385.6	498.2
Total	8,260.8	8,802.1	9,736.1	10,732.9	11,750.5	12,686.0	13,604.7

TABLE 10.2
Projected Chinese Citizen Population
by Sex and Age Group, 2005–2035

Age Group	2005	2010	2015	2020	2025	2030	2035
				Male			
0–4	258.8	276.3	278.6	274.8	266.2	258.5	253.0
5–9	249.4	238.3	275.7	278.0	274.3	265.7	254.4
10–14	272.1	240.2	258.0	275.5	277.8	274.0	265.5
15–19	260.9	271.7	239.9	257.7	275.2	277.5	273.7
20–24	273.3	250.5	271.3	239.5	257.4	274.8	277.1
25–29	249.7	272.6	259.9	270.7	239.0	256.8	274.2
30–34	227.8	248.9	271.7	259.1	269.9	238.3	256.0
35–39	230.7	226.7	247.7	270.5	257.9	268.6	237.2
40–44	235.3	228.8	224.9	245.8	268.4	255.9	266.6
45–49	225.2	232.3	226.0	222.2	242.8	265.2	252.9
50–54	192.1	220.3	227.5	221.5	217.8	238.0	259.9
55–59	162.2	185.4	213.0	220.1	214.3	210.7	230.2
60–64	108.7	152.5	184.0	200.9	207.6	202.1	198.7
65–69	91.5	98.2	138.1	167.1	182.4	188.4	183.5
70–74	50.2	77.2	83.1	117.3	141.9	154.9	160.0
75 & Over	56.6	74.6	107.1	133.3	176.6	223.5	263.8
Total	3,144.5	3,324.5	3,506.5	3,654.0	3,769.5	3,852.9	3,906.7
				Female			
0–4	240.4	255.4	257.1	253.5	245.6	238.5	233.4
5–9	235.1	240.2	255.2	257.0	253.4	245.4	235.0
10–14	250.3	235.0	240.0	255.1	256.8	253.2	245.3
15–19	246.2	250.1	234.8	239.9	254.9	256.7	253.0
20–24	259.3	245.9	249.7	234.5	239.6	254.6	256.3
25–29	240.1	258.8	245.4	249.3	234.1	239.2	254.1
30–34	222.7	239.4	258.1	244.8	248.7	233.5	238.5
35–39	224.5	221.7	238.4	257.0	243.7	247.6	232.5
40–44	231.5	222.9	220.2	236.8	255.2	242.1	245.9
45–49	214.9	228.9	220.5	217.9	234.3	252.6	239.6
50–54	178.5	211.8	225.8	217.5	214.9	231.1	249.2
55–59	145.7	172.5	205.0	218.8	210.8	208.3	224.0
60–64	99.8	139.5	165.5	197.0	210.2	202.5	200.1
65–69	88.5	92.2	129.1	153.4	182.7	195.0	187.8
70–74	55.3	77.2	80.4	112.8	134.0	159.5	170.2
75 & Over	77.4	95.7	125.7	148.8	190.2	234.9	285.5
Total	3,010.2	3,187.2	3,350.9	3,494.1	3,609.1	3,694.7	3,750.4

TABLE 10.3

Projected Indian Citizen Population
by Sex and Age Group, 2005–2035

Age Group	2005	2010	2015	2020	2025	2030	2035
				Male			
0–4	85.1	95.2	96.9	96.5	94.5	92.6	92.4
5–9	87.4	84.5	94.8	96.6	96.3	94.3	92.4
10–14	88.5	87.2	84.4	94.3	96.5	96.2	94.2
15–19	86.4	88.3	87.0	84.2	94.2	96.4	96.1
20–24	87.6	86.0	87.9	86.7	84.1	94.1	96.2
25–29	77.1	87.1	85.7	87.7	86.5	83.8	93.8
30–34	70.6	76.6	86.7	85.3	87.3	86.2	83.6
35–39	66.7	70.0	76.1	86.2	84.8	87.3	85.8
40–44	67.7	65.9	69.3	75.4	85.4	84.2	86.6
45–49	62.7	66.4	64.8	68.3	74.4	84.4	83.1
50–54	47.6	60.8	64.6	63.2	66.7	72.7	82.6
55–59	36.3	45.3	58.1	62.0	60.9	64.4	70.3
60–64	18.4	33.5	42.1	54.3	58.1	57.2	60.8
65–69	15.1	16.3	29.8	37.7	48.8	52.5	51.8
70–74	9.3	12.4	13.5	24.9	31.6	41.2	44.4
75 & Over	10.2	12.9	17.1	20.8	35.6	46.9	61.8
Total	916.7	988.4	1,058.8	1,124.1	1,185.7	1,234.4	1,275.9
				Female			
0–4	81.4	89.0	90.5	90.1	88.3	86.6	86.8
5–9	83.4	81.0	88.7	90.3	90.0	88.2	86.5
10–14	86.3	83.2	80.9	88.6	90.2	90.0	88.2
15–19	82.6	86.1	83.1	80.4	88.5	90.1	89.9
20–24	86.1	82.3	85.8	82.9	80.2	88.3	89.0
25–29	80.4	85.7	82.0	85.6	82.7	80.1	88.2
30–34	72.0	79.9	85.3	81.7	85.3	82.5	79.9
35–39	68.6	71.5	79.5	84.9	81.3	84.9	82.1
40–44	68.9	67.9	70.9	78.8	84.2	80.7	84.4
45–49	62.7	67.9	67.0	70.0	77.9	83.3	79.9
50–54	48.6	61.3	66.5	65.7	68.9	76.8	82.2
55–59	35.6	46.9	59.4	64.5	63.4	66.5	74.4
60–64	19.3	33.7	44.5	56.5	61.1	60.6	63.8
65–69	18.4	17.6	30.8	41.0	52.0	56.9	56.1
70–74	12.0	15.7	15.2	26.7	35.6	45.3	49.6
75 & Over	11.8	16.9	23.3	27.6	39.6	54.8	72.9
Total	918.1	986.6	1,053.4	1,115.3	1,169.7	1,215.6	1,253.9

stage by 6.76 per cent. The total population for Malaysia calculated from the two-stage procedure is shown in Table 10.4. It should be pointed out that we do not have the projected total population by sex and quinary age group.

The amount of population increase for every five-year period is expected to indicate a rising trend during the first fifteen years, moving up from 241,200 during 2005–2010 to the high of 2,681,200 during 2015–2020. Thereafter, a reversal is expected to appear as a continuous downtrend will occur during the second fifteen years. The amount of population increase will commence to shrink progressively, being reduced from the peak of 2,681,200 during 2015–2020 to the lower figure of 2,211,500 during the last five-year period 2030–2035. The implied annual rate of population growth will exhibit a deceleration from 1.7 per cent to 1.1 per cent towards the end of the thirty-year period.

TABLE 10.4

Projected Total Population, 2005–2035

Year	Projected Population ('000)	Increase	
		Number ('000)	Annual Growth Rate (%)
2005	26,127.7	—	—
2010	28,541.9	2,414.2	1.7
2015	31,156.8	2,614.9	1.7
2020	33,838.0	2,681.2	1.6
2025	36,476.1	2,638.1	1.4
2030	38,854.5	2,378.1	1.3
2035	41,066.0	2,211.5	1.1

Overall, the population of Malaysia is expected to expand by some 15 million or 36.4 per cent from 26 million in 2005 to 41 million in thirty years' time in 2035. What this means is that there will be 65 years left for the population to be augmented by 29 million in order to achieve the original aim of having a population of 70 million in the year 2100. The possibility of attaining this national target in such a remote future is rather uncertain but not impossible, even though a deceleration in the annual rate of population growth is expected to take place in the years ahead. As mentioned earlier, Malaysia has in fact abandoned in December 2004 its target of having 70 million by 2100.

It would be interesting to proceed a step further by examining the differences in the future growth of the population among the three

ethnic groups as depicted in Table 10.5. It is necessary to emphasise
again that the projected population of these three ethnic groups refers to
the citizen population only and not to the total population (citizens and
non-citizens) as in our previous analysis of the total population of
Malaysia. The figures given in the table reveal that these three ethnic
groups are expected to share the common experience of a slowing down
in the rate of population increase in the coming years.

TABLE 10.5
Projected Citizen Population for
Three Main Ethnic Groups, 2005–2035

Year	Citizen Population ('000)	Increase	
		Number ('000)	Annual Growth Rate (%)
Bumiputeras			
2005	16,060.4	—	—
2010	17,785.7	1,725.3	2.1
2015	19,709.8	1,924.1	2.1
2020	21,760.5	2,050.7	2.0
2025	23,841.7	2,081.2	1.9
2030	25,767.4	1,925.7	1.4
2035	27,613.8	1,846.4	0.9
Chinese			
2005	6,154.9	—	—
2010	6,511.7	356.8	1.1
2015	6,857.4	345.7	1.0
2020	7,148.1	290.7	0.8
2025	7,378.6	230.5	0.7
2030	7,547.6	169.0	0.5
2035	7,657.1	109.5	0.2
Indians			
2005	1,834.8	—	—
2010	1,975.2	140.4	1.5
2015	2,112.2	137.0	1.4
2020	2,239.4	127.2	1.2
2025	2,355.4	116.0	1.0
2030	2,450.0	94.6	0.8
2035	2,529.8	79.8	0.7

The deceleration in the annual growth rate of the citizen population is expected to be the slowest among the Bumiputeras, with the rate falling from 2.1 per cent during 2005–20 to 0.9 per cent towards the end of the projected period in 2030–2035. In contrast, the Chinese will experience the fastest deceleration in their growth rate which is projected to fall from 1.1 per cent during 2005–2010 to the low of 0.2 per cent during the last five-year period. As for the Indians, the deceleration in their growth rate is just slightly less than the Chinese; their rate falling from 1.5 per cent at the beginning to 0.7 per cent at the end of the period.

FUTURE POPULATION STRUCTURE

The recent changes in the ethnic composition of the Malaysian population has engendered some public interest in view of the attendant political and economic implications. In the main, the concern has emanated from the Chinese and Indian communities who see their political influence being diminished by the continuous fall in their proportion of the total population. The future shift in the ethnic composition in favour of the Bumiputera population at the expense of the other communities will certainly continue to attract public attention, more so if we confine our analysis to only the citizen population as depicted in Table 10.6. Obviously, only citizens are empowered to participate in State and Federal elections.

TABLE 10.6
Percentage Distribution of Projected Citizen Population
by Main Ethnic Groups, 2005–2035

Year	Bumiputeras	Chinese	Indians	Others	Total
2005	65.9	25.3	7.5	1.3	100.0
2010	66.8	24.5	7.4	1.3	100.0
2015	67.8	23.6	7.3	1.3	100.0
2020	69.0	22.7	7.1	1.3	100.0
2025	70.1	21.7	6.9	1.3	100.0
2030	71.1	20.8	6.8	1.3	100.0
2035	72.1	20.0	6.6	1.3	100.0

The changes in the ethnic citizen population resulting from the differences in the future population growth among these ethnic groups discussed earlier are laid out in the table. Consequent on a relatively more rapid growth rate, the Bumiputera citizen population is expected to enlarge from 65.9 per cent in 2005 to 72.1 per cent in 2035. In contrast, the share of the Chinese citizen population will fall continuously from one-fourth (25.3 per cent) to one-fifth (20.0 per cent) during the same period. The proportion of Indian citizen population will also experience a clear downtrend, down from 7.5 per cent to 6.6 per cent.

Another important aspect of the future changes in the population structure that can be revealed by the results of our population projection is the process of population ageing.[10] As in countries that have been experiencing the ageing of their population, the ageing of the Malaysian population has commenced to take place on account of the decline in fertility.[11] The growth in the number of old people aged 60 and over has

TABLE 10.7

**Projected Citizen Population Aged 60 and Over
for Three Ethnic Groups, 2005–2035**

Year	Citizen Population Aged 60 & Over ('000)	Ten-Year Increase		Percentage of Total Citizen Population
		Number ('000)	Percentage	
Bumiputeras				
2005	985.9	—	—	6.0
2015	1,599.9	614.0	62.3	8.1
2025	2,529.4	929.5	58.1	10.6
2035	3,929.7	1,400.3	55.4	14.3
Chinese				
2005	628.0	—	—	10.2
2015	1,013.0	385.0	61.4	14.8
2025	1,425.6	412.6	40.7	19.3
2035	1,649.6	224.0	15.7	21.5
Indians				
2005	114.5	—	—	6.2
2015	216.3	101.8	88.9	10.2
2025	352.9	136.6	63.2	15.0
2035	461.2	108.3	30.7	18.2

always posed serious challenges to countries to adopt and plan to meet the needs of an older population.

It may be recalled that we have not prepared any projection for the total population of Malaysia by quinary age group, and hence we are not able to study the ageing of the overall population. What we have are the data that can allow us to make a comparative analysis of ageing among the citizen population of the three main ethnic groups. Table 10.7 shows that the Bumiputera citizen population aged 60 and over is expected to expand by four-fold during the projection period, up from 995,900 in 2005 of 3,929,700 in 2035. The same period will witness the Chinese citizen population aged 60 and over expanding by two-and-a-half times and the Indian citizen population aged 60 and over by four times. The former is expected to be enlarged from 628,000 to 1,649,600 and the latter from 114,500 to 461,200.

What is perhaps more significant is the proportion of people aged 60 and over to the total population within each ethnic group. The proportion of elderly people in the Bumiputera citizen population stood at the low of 6.0 per cent in 2005, and is expected to rise steadily to 14.3 per cent at the end of the period. The proportion of old people in the Indian citizen population also began at the low of 6.2 per cent, but is expected to rise faster to reach 18.2 per cent in 2035. The Chinese citizen population, which has experienced a fertility decline earlier and more rapidly, had a higher proportion (10.2 per cent) of old people at the start of the period, and is expected to continue to see this proportion become bigger to reach the high of 21.5 per cent in 2035.

CONCLUSION

The results of any population projection will be as good as the assumptions employed in the computation turning out to be true in the future. Experience has shown that the future path of migration, mortality and fertility rarely adhere to the assumptions adopted in calculating the population projection. At best, the results of our population projection will serve to provide a general idea of the changes to the population that will take place in the next three decades.

Notes

1. See, for example, "Target: 70 Million", *Malaysia Business*, May 1984, and "Malaysia Moves on Major Boost to Population", *Asian Wall Street Journal*, 10 April 1984.

2. Abdullah bin Ayob (Chairman), *Towards a Population of Seventy Million* (Kuala Lumpur: National Population and Family Development Board, 1984).
3. *Asiaweek*, 20 April 1984.
4. *Malaysian Business Times*, 3 August 1984.
5. *Population Headliners*, ESCAP, No. 124, July 1985.
6. *New Straits Times*, 20 October 1984.
7. *Straits Times*, 7 August 1985.
8. "Scrapped: Target for Population of 70 Million", *Straits Times*, 11 December 2004.
9. United Nations, *Methods of Population Projections by Sex and Age* (New York: Department of Economic and Social Affairs, 1956).
10. Malaysia, *2000 Population and Housing Censuses of Malaysia, Monograph Series No. 1: Population Ageing Trends in Malaysia* (Kuala Lumpur: Department of Statistics, 2005).
11. Saw Swee-Hock, "The Dynamics of Ageing in Singapore's Population, *Annal of the Academy of Medicine* 14, no. 4 (October 1985).

Bibliography

CENSUS REPORTS

Chander, R., *1970 Population and Housing Census of Malaysia*, Kuala Lumpur: Department of Statistics.
  (1) Vol. 1: General Population Tables
          Part 1. Perlis (1971)
               2. Penang and Province Wellesley (1972)
               3. Malacca (1972)
               4. Negri Sembilan (1972)
               5. Selangor (1972)
               6. Pahang (1972)
               7. Trengganu (1972)
               8. Kelantan (1972)
               9. Perak (1972)
             10. Kedah (1972)
             11. Johore (1972)

  (2) Vol. 2: General Housing Tables — Towns, Villages and Local Council Areas
          Part 1. Perlis (1972)
               2. Penang and Province Wellesley (1972)
               3. Malacca (1972)
               4. Negri Sembilan (1972)
               5. Selangor (1972)
               6. Pahang (1972)
               7. Trengganu (1972)
               8. Kelantan (1972)
               9. Perak (1972)
             10. Kedah (1973)
             11. Johore (1973)

    12.   Sarawak (1973)
    13.   Sabah (1973)

  (3)   Field Count Summary (1971)
  (4)   Urban Conurbations — Population and Households in Ten Gazetted
        Towns and their Adjoining Built-up Areas (1971)
  (5)   Community Groups (1972)
  (6)   West Malaysia Census of Housing Final Report (1973)
  (7)   Age Distribution (1973)
  (8)   An Interim Report on the Post-Enumeration Survey (1973)
  (9)   Map Showing Distribution of Population (1974)

Haji Aziz bin Othman, *2000 General Report of the Population and Housing Census*
(Kuala Lumpur: Department of Statistics, 2005).

Khoo Soo Gim, *Population and Housing Census of Malaysia 1991*, Kuala Lumpur:
    Department of Statistics.
  (1)   Preliminary Count Report (1991)
  (2)   Preliminary Count Report for Urban and Rural Areas (1991)
  (3)   Mukim Preliminary Count Report (1992)
  (4)   Preliminary Count Report for Local Authority Areas (1992)
  (5)   Vol. 1: General Report of the Population Census (1995)
  (6)   Vol. 2: General Report of the Population Census (1995)
  (7)   General Report of the Housing Census (1995)
  (8)   Population Report for Administrative Districts (1995)
  (9)   State Population Report
        1.   Johore (1995)
        2.   Kedah (1995)
        3.   Selangor (1995)
        4.   Wilayah Persekutuan Kuala Lumpur (1995)
        5.   Penang (1995)
        6.   Melaka (1995)
        7.   Perak (1995)
        8.   Negri Sembilan (1995)
        9.   Sabah (1995)
       10.   Pahang (1996)
       11.   Terengganu (1996)
       12.   Wilayah Persekutuan Labuan (1996)
       13.   Perlis (1996)
       14.   Kelantan (1996)
       15.   Sarawak (1996)

(10) State Housing Report
  1. Johore (1996)
  2. Kedah (1996)
  3. Selangor (1996)
  4. Wilayah Persekutuan Kuala Lumpur (1996)
  5. Penang (1996)
  6. Melaka 1996)
  7. Sabah (1996)
  8. Pahang (1996)
  9. Wilayah Persekutuan Labuan (1996)
  10. Perlis (1996)
  11. Kelantan (1996)
  12. Sarawak (1996)
  13. Perak (1996)
  14. Negri Sembilan (1996)
  15. Terengganu (1996)
(11) Population Report for Mukim (1996)
(12) Evaluation of Coverage and Content Errors of the 1991 Population Census (1996)
(13) Population Report for Local Authority Areas (1996)
(14) Census Map (1996)
(15) Population Report for Administrative Districts: Occupation and Industry (1996)

Khoo Teik Huat, *1980 Population and Housing Census of Malaysia*, Kuala Lumpur: Department of Statistics.
(1) Preliminary Field Count Summary (1980)
(2) Preliminary Field Count Summaries (1982)
(3) Census of Housing, Malaysia 1980: Summary Report (1982)
(4) General Report of the Housing Census of Malaysia, Vol. 1 (1983)
(5) General Report of the Housing Census of Malaysia, Vol. 2 (1983)
(6) Vol. 1: General Report of the Population Census (1983)
(7) Vol. 2: General Report of the Population Census (1983)
(8) State Population Report
  1. Kelantan (1983)
  2. Sabah (1983)
  3. Sarawak 1983)
  4. Selangor 1983)
  5. Pulau Pinang (1983)
  6. Perlis (1984)
  7. Johor (1984)

8. Perak (1984)
9. Kedah (1984)
10. Negri Sembilan (1984)
11. Pahang (1984)
12. Melaka (1984)
(9) State Housing Report
1. Sabah (1984)
2. Selangor (1984)
3. Kelantan (1984)
4. Wilayah Persekutuan (1984)
5. Sarawak (1984)
6. Pulau Pinang (1984)
7. Pahang (1984)
8. Terengganu (1984)
9. Johor (1984)
10. Perlis (1984)
11. Perak (1984)
12. Negri Sembilan (1984)
(10) Population Report for Administrative Districts: Age, Ethnicity, Sex, Households (1984)
(11) Population Report for Administrative Districts: Occupation, Industry (1984)
(12) Report on the Post Enumeration Survey 1980 (1985)
(13) Population Report for Local Authority Areas: Age, Ethnicity, Sex, Households, Economic Activity, Education (1986)

Shaari bin Abdul Rahman, *2000 Population and Housing Census of Malaysia*, Kuala Lumpur: Department of Statistics.
(1) Preliminary Count Report (2000)
(2) Preliminary Count Report for Urban and Rural Areas (2001)
(3) Population Distribution and Basic Demographic Characteristics (2001)
(4) Population Distribution by Local Authority Areas and Mukims (2001)
(5) Education and Social Characteristics of the Population (2002)
(6) Economic Characteristics of the Population (2003)
(7) Characteristics of Living Quarters (2003)
(8) Migration and Population Distribution (2004)
(9) Household Characteristics (2004)

OTHER OFFICIAL PUBLICATIONS

Attorney-General's Chambers, *Malaysia: Immigration Laws* (Kuala Lumpur: Government Printer, 1963).
Malaysia, *Family, Planning Act 1996*, No. 42 of 1966, Warta Kerajaan: Seri Paduka Baginda. Kuala Lumpur, 12 May 1966.

_____, *Revised Intercensal Population Estimates, Malaysia: For Peninsular Malaysia, 1957–1970, Sabah and Sarawak, 1960–1970* (Kuala Lumpur: Department of Statistics, 1974).

_____, *Revised Mid-Year Estimates of the Population by Age, Sex and Ethnic Group for Peninsular Malaysia, Sabah and Sarawak, 1970–1980*, Studies on Demography and Population Subjects, No. 2 (Kuala Lumpur: Department of Statistics, 1986).

_____, *Revised Intercensal Mid-Year Population Estimates, Malaysia, 1981–1990* (Kuala Lumpur: Department of Statistics, July 1997).

_____, *Current Population Estimates: Peninsular Malaysia, 1984–* (Kuala Lumpur: Department of Statistics. Published annually).

_____, *Current Population Estimates: Sabah and Sarawak, 1984–* (Kuala Lumpur: Department of Statistics. Published annually).

_____, *Demographic Estimates for Sabah and Sarawak 1970–80*, Studies on Demography and Population Subjects, No. 1 (Kuala Lumpur: Department of Statistics, 1986).

_____, *Quarterly Review of Malaysian Population Statistics for the years 1986–1999* (Kuala Lumpur: Department of Statistics).

_____, *Yearbook of Statistics Malaysia, for the years 1970–2006* (Kuala Lumpur: Department of Statistics).

_____, *Monthly Statistical Bulletin, for the years 1970–2006* (Kuala Lumpur: Department of Statistics).

_____, *Social Statistics Bulletin, Malaysia, for the years 1980–2006* (Kuala Lumpur: Department of Statistics).

_____, *Labour Force Survey, for the years 1970 to 2005* (Kuala Lumpur: Department of Statistics).

_____, *Migration Survey Report, Malaysia, 1992/93, 1995–1997, 1999–2002*, Kuala Lumpur: Department of Statistics.

_____, *Rubber Statistics Handbook, 2005* (Kuala Lumpur: Department of Statistics, 2006).

_____, *Vital Statistics, Malaysia, for the years 1970 to 2003* (Kuala Lumpur: Department of Statistics).

_____, *Vital Statistics Time Series, Malaysia, 1963–1998* (Kuala Lumpur: Department of Statistics, 2001).

_____, *2000 Population and Housing Census of Malaysia*, Monograph Series No. 1, *Population Ageing Trends in Malaysia* (Kuala Lumpur: Department of Statistics, 2005).

_____, *Report of the Registrar-General on Population, Births, Deaths, Marriages and Adoptions* (Kuala Lumpur: Registration Department, 1981).

_____, *Second Malaysia Plan 1971–1975* (Kuala Lumpur: Government Printer, 1971).

_____, *Third Malaysia Plan 1976–1980* (Kuala Lumpur: Government Printer, 1976).

_____, *Annual Report of National Population and Family Development Board, 1966-2004* (Kuala Lumpur: Ministry of National Unity and Social Development.

Marjoribanks, N.E. and A.K.G. Ahmad Tambi Marakkaya, *Report on Indian Labour Emigration to Ceylon and Malaya* (Madras: Government Press, 1917).

Parr, C.W.C., *Report of Protector of Chinese 1914* (Singapore: Government Press, 1915).

Straits Settlements, *Annual Report on the Administration of the Straits Settlements, 1860-1861* (Singapore: Government Press).

_____, *Report of Protector of Chinese, for the years 1914-1932* (Singapore: Government Press).

_____, *Report of the Immigration Department, 1933* (Singapore: Government Press, 1935).

Straits Settlements and Federated Malay States, *Report on Indian Immigration, 1910* (Singapore: Government Press, 1912).

_____, *Report of the Immigration Department 1938* (Singapore: Government Press, 1940).

BOOKS

Ahmad Ibrahim, *Law and Population in Malaysia* (Medford: Law and Population Programme, Fletcher School of Law and Diplomacy, 1977).

_____, *Family Law in Malaysia and Singapore*, 2nd Edition (Singapore: Malayan Law Journal, 1984).

_____, *Law of Marriage and Divorce* (Malaysia) (Tokyo: Printed by Nihon Kajyo Pub. Co., published between 1982 and 1985).

Abdullah bin Ayob, *Towards a Population of Seventy Million* (Kuala Lumpur: National Population and Family Development Board, 1984).

Andaya, Babara Watson and Leonard Y. Andaya, *A History of Malaysia* (Honolulu: University of Hawaii Press, 2001).

Braddell, T., *Statistics of the British Possessions in the Straits of Malacca* (Penang: Penang Gazette Printing Office, 1861).

Djamour, Judith, *The Muslim Matrimonial Court in Singapore* (London: Athlone Press, 1966).

Geoghegan, J. *Note on Emigration from India* (Calcutta: Government Press, 1873).

Hall, D.G.E., *A History of Southeast Asia* (London: Macmillan, 1958).

Hooker, M.B., *Islamic Law in South-East Asia* (Oxford University Press, 1984).

Jackson, R.N., *Immigrant Labour and Development of Malaya* (Kuala Lumpur: Government Printer, 1961).

Jones, L.W., *The Population of Borneo: A Study of the Peoples of Sarawak, Sabah and Brunei* (London: Athlone Press, 1966).

Lee Yong Leng, *Population and Settlement in Sarawak* (Singapore: Donald Moore, 1970).

Leete, Richard, *Malaysia's Demographic Transition: Rapid Development, Culture and Politics* (Kuala Lumpur: Oxford University Press, 1996).

Lim Heng Kow, *The Evolution of the Urban System in Malaya* (Kuala Lumpur: Universiti Malaya Press, 1978).

Maimunah Aminuddin, *An A-Z of Malaysian Employment Law*, Kuala Lumpur and New York, McGraw Hill, 1999.

Newbold, T.J., *Political and Statistical Account of the British Settlement in the Straits of Malacca*, Vol. 1 (London: John Murray, 1939).

Nik Noriani Nik Badlishah, *Marriage and Divorce under Islamic Law* (Kuala Lumpur: International Law Book Services, 1998).

_____, *Marriage and Divorce: Law Reform within Islamic Framework* (Kuala Lumpur: International Law Book Services, 2000).

Nor Laily Aziz, *Malaysia: Population and Development* (Kuala Lumpur: National Family Planning Board, 1981).

Nor Laily Aziz, Tan Boon Ann Ramli Othman and Kuan Lin Chee, *Facts and Figures: Malaysia National Population and Family Development* (Kuala Lumpur: National Family Planning Board, 1982).

Parmer, Norman, *Colonial Labour Policy and Administration* (New York: Association for Asian Studies, 1960).

Porrith, Vernon, L., *British Colonial Rule in Sarawak, 1946–1963* (Kuala Lumpur: Oxford University Press, 1997).

Purcell, Victor, *The Chinese in Southeast Asia* (London: Oxford University Press, 1951).

Ranjit, S., *The Making of Sabah, 1865–1941* (Kuala Lumpur: University of Malaya Press, 2000).

Rasamani Kandiah, *Marriage and Dissolution Handbook*, MLJ Handbook Series (Kuala Lumpur: Malayan Law Journal 2003).

Saw Swee-Hock, *Estimation of Interstate Migration in Peninsular Malaysia, 1947–1970* (Singapore: Institute of Southeast Asian Studies, 1980).

_____, *Changing Labour Force of Malaysia* (Manila: Council for Asian Manpower Studies, 1985).

_____, *The Population of Peninsular Malaysia* (Singapore: Singapore University Press, 1988).

_____, *Bibliography of Malaysian Demography* (Singapore: Institute of Southeast Asian Studies, 2005).

Turnbull, C. Mary, *A History of Malaysia, Singapore and Brunei* (London: Allen & Unwin, 1989).

United Nations, *Methods of Population Projections by Sex and Age* (New York: Department of Economic and Social Affairs, 1956).

_____, *Handbook of Population Census Methods, Volume 11: Economic*

Characteristics of Population. Series F, No. 5, Rev. 1, Studies in Method (New York, 1958).

_____, *Manual VI: Methods of Measuring Internal Migration* (New York: Department of International Economic and Social Affairs, 1970.

Zaleha, Kamaruddin, *Introduction to Divorce Laws in Malaysia* (Kuala Lumpur: International Islamic University Malaysia Cooperative, 1998).

_____, *Islamic Family Law Issues 2000* (Kuala Lumpur: International Islamic University Malaysia Cooperative, 1998).

ARTICLES

Abdul Razak bin Hussein, "Government Policy on Birth Control in Malaysia", *Kajian Ekonomi Malaysia* 3, no. 1 (June 1966).

Ahmad Ibrahim, "Islam/Customary Law — Malaysia", *Intisari*, 2(2): 47–72 (1965).

_____, "Developments in Marriage Laws in Malaysia and Singapore", *Malaya Law Review* 2, no. 2 (December 1970).

Blythe, W.L., "Historical Sketch of Chinese Labour in Malaya", *Journal of the Malayan Branch of the Royal Asiatic Society* 20, Part 1 (June 1947).

Chong, Terence, "The Emerging Politics of Islam Hadhari" in *Malaysia: Recent Trends and Challenges*, edited by Saw Swee-Hock and K. Kesavapany (Singapore: Institute of Southeast Asian Studies, 2005).

Dixon, Ruth B., "Explaining Cross-Cultural Variations in Age at Marriage and Proportion Never Marrying", *Population Studies* 25, no. 1 (July 1971).

Dobby, E.H.G., "Settlement Patterns in Malaya", *Geographical Review* 32, no. 2 (April 1942).

Gordon, Shirle, "Malay Marriage/Divorce in the Eleven States of Malaya and Singapore", *Intisari* 2, no. 2 (n.d.).

Hajnal, John, "Age at Marriage and Proportion Marrying", *Population Studies* 7, no. 2 (November 1953).

Huang, K.K. "Malayan Immigration Law and Malayan Chinese", *China Weekly Review* 62 (October 1932).

Lee Hock Guan, "Globalization and Ethnic Integration in Malaysia", in *Malaysia Recent Trends and Challenge*, edited by Saw Swee-Hock and K. Kesavapany (Singapore: Institute of Southeast Asian Studies, 2005).

Mohamed Din Bin Ali, "Malay Customary Law and Family", *Intisari* 2, no. 2 (1965).

Mohamed Khir Johari, "National Family Planning Board: Chairman's Inaugural Address", *Kajian Ekonomi Malaysia* 3, no. 1 (June 1966).

Pryor, R.J., "Law of Migration?: The Experience of Malaysia and Other Countries", *Geographica* 5 (1969).

Rafiah Salam, "The Legal Status of Women in a Multi-Racial Malaysian Society", in Hing Ai Yun et. al. (eds.), *Women in Malaysia* (Kuala Lumpur: Pelanduk Publications, 1984).

Ravenstein, E.G., "The Law of Migration", *Journal of the Royal Statistical Society* (June 1879).

Saw Swee-Hock, "Trends and Differentials in International Migration in Malaya", *Ekonomi* 4, no. 1 (December 1963).

_____, "Regional Differences in the Structure of the Labour Force in Malaysia", *Kajian Ekonomi Malaysia* 3, no. 2 (December 1966).

_____, "The Structure of the Labour Force in Malaya", *International Labour Review* 98, no. 1 (July 1968).

_____, "Urbanization in West Malaysia, 1911–70" in *Towards a Modern Asia: Aim, Resources and Strategies*, edited by Lim Teck Ghee and Vincent Lowe (Kuala Lumpur: Heinemann Educational Books, 1976).

_____, "The Dynamics of Ageing in Singapore's Population", *Annals of the Academy of Medicine* 14, no. 4 (October 1985).

_____, "Population and Labour Force Growth and Patterns in ASEAN Countries", *Philippine Review of Economics and Business* 25, nos. 3 & 4 (September and December 1988).

_____, "Ethnic Fertility Differentials in Peninsular Malaysia and Singapore", *Journal of Biosocial Science* 22, no. 1 (January 1999).

_____, "Population Trends and Patterns in Multiracial Malaysia" in *Malaysia: Recent Trends and Challenges*, edited by Saw Swee-Hock and K. Kesavapany (Singapore: Institute of Southeast Asian Studies, 2005).

Peter C. Smith, "Asian Marriage Patterns in Transition", *Journal of Family History* 5, no. 1 (1980).

NEWSPAPERS

Asian Wall Street Journal
Business Times
International Herald Tribune
Malaysian Business Times
New Paper Today
New Straits Times
STAR
Straits Times

Index

www.ingramcontent.com/pod-product-compliance
Lightning Source LLC
Chambersburg PA
CBHW021541260326
41914CB00001B/106